PRIVATE PRESLEY

THE MISSING YEARS—ELVIS IN GERMANY

ANDREAS SCHRÖER

William Morrow and Company, Inc.
New York

First published in Great Britain in 1993 by Boxtree Limited

Thanks to the following photo agencies who supplied supplementary photos for this book:
Associated Press–Pages 8, 9, 11, 13, 16, 27, 28, 29, 35, 92, 144
Topham Picture Library–Pages 10, 11, 12, 14, 17, 25, 35, 66, 67, 75, 78, 144
Syndication International–Pages 12, 14, 32, 153
The Hulton Picture Library–Pages 46, 122, 123, 152, 158
London Features International–Page 5

ACKNOWLEDGMENTS

Most of the information contained in this book has been compiled over the years from various sources in Germany, including press cuttings and personal interviews, by Andreas Schröer, Michael Knorr, and Oskar Hentschel.

The following English-language books were a secondary source of information. *Elvis the Soldier* (Collectors Service GmbH, Bamberg, 1983) by Rex and Elisabeth Mansfield. *Private Elvis* (Fey Verlags GmbH, Stuttgart, 1978) by Diego Cortez, with photographs by Rudolf Paulini. *Operation Elvis* (André Deutsch, London, 1960) by Alan Levy. *Elvis and Me* (Putnam's, New York, 1985) by Priscilla Beaulieu Presley with Sandra Harmon. *Elvis: What Happened?* (Ballantine, New York, 1977; William Collins, London, 1977) by Red West, Sonny West and Dave Hebler, as told to Steve Dunleavy. *Elvis, We Love You Tender* (Delacorte Press, New York, 1980; New English Library, London, 1980) by Dee Presley, Billy, Rick and David Stanley, as told to Martin Torgoff. *Elvis* (McGraw-Hill, New York, 1981) by Albert Goldman. *Elvis and Gladys* (MacMillan, New York, 1985; Weidenfeld & Nicolson, London, 1985) by Elaine Dundy. *Elvis* (Simon & Schuster, New York, 1971; Abacus, London, 1978) by Jerry Hopkins.

Thanks are due to Bob Turner of the London *Daily Mirror* library.

The German-English translations were by Ursula Mayer Harbinson.

Merlin would like to thank the following for their help in making this book possible:
Ray Santilli, Margaret and Luke, Gary Shoefield, Sharon and Luke, Joe Toledano, Lara Friedland, Kevin Allen, Sandra Boyer, Harry Maguire, Jean Short, Graham Hart, Sarah Mahaffy, Adrian Sington, Rod Green.

It is the policy of William Morrow and Company, Inc., and its imprints and affiliates, recognizing the importance of preserving what has been written, to print the books we publish on acid-free paper, and we exert our best efforts to that end.

Library of Congress Cataloging-in-Publication Data

Schröer, Andreas.
     Private Presley: the missing years, Elvis in Germany/Andreas
    Schröer.
        p.   cm.
     ISBN 0-688-04609-6
     1. Presley, Elvis, 1935–1977.   2. Singers—Travel—Germany (West).
   I. Title.
   ML420.P96S37   1993   93-17503
   782.42166′092—dc20   CIP
   [B]   MN

Printed in the United States of America

First U.S. Edition

1 2 3 4 5 6 7 8 9 10

BOOK DESIGN BY NIGEL DAVIES, TITAN STUDIO

MEMORABILIA PHOTOGRAPHED BY PAUL FORRESTER

CONTENTS

THE JORDANAIRES

I have a lot of great memories of Elvis during the years of his Army tenure in Germany.

After he completed eight weeks of basic training at Ft. Hood, Texas, Elvis was granted a two week leave. On June 10-11, 1958 The Jordanaires, along with musicians Hank Garland, Chet Atkins, Bob Moore, Floyd Cramer, Buddy Harman and D. J. Fontana joined Elvis at RCA's Nashville studio to record the five songs that were to be his last of the 1950s - *I Need Your Love Tonight*, *A Big Hunk O' Love*, *Ain't That Lovin' You Baby*, *A Fool Such As I* and *I Got Stung*. Elvis was always concerned about his fans, but now he wondered if he would have any fans left when he returned.

I saw him one more time before he left for Germany. My wife, Jean, and I were visiting at Graceland in Memphis and he asked us to go with him to the Reserve Headquarters where he had to take care of some last minute details. During these last moments we spent with Elvis, it was obvious that he was afraid his career was over. WE ASSURED HIM IT WASN'T.

I give Colonel Parker a lot of credit for keeping Elvis's name in front of the public while he was in the service.

We kept in close touch with him the eighteen months he was in

Germany. Among other things, I sent him an album by the black spiritual group *The Harmonizing Four*. When I finally saw him after his return, I asked him if he liked it. He said, "Are you kidding? I wore it out!"

The only other time I saw him while he was in the service was when his mother died in August 1958. D. J. Fontana, Neal Matthews and I drove to Memphis the day of her funeral. I'll never forget entering Graceland and seeing Elvis sitting on the steps in the entry hall crying his heart out. It was one of the saddest things I'd ever seen.

I know Elvis enjoyed the Army, basically he liked the German people. He enjoyed being with German girls and, of course, it was while he was in Germany that he met Priscilla, who was stationed there with her father.

There's one thing we shall always treasure of the fifteen years we worked with Elvis . . . we were sitting around eating during a recording session at Radio Recorders in Hollywood. He looked at us and said, "if there had not been The Jordanaires, I guess there would not have been a *me*." We said, "What . . . you can't mean that." He said, "Yep, you guys took an interest in me and when I didn't care, you helped me with bad material (*referring to the movie songs*) and just when I did not want to record." We did it because of our love for him.

Gordon Stoker

PRIVATE
PRESLEY

Introduction

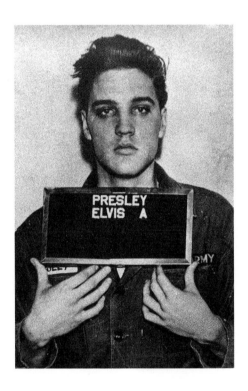

When Elvis Presley exploded onto the music scene in 1956, he outraged conservative America. The more Elvis shocked adults, the more teenagers loved him. Soon he was the most popular and the most reviled singer in the world - an exciting sexual and musical taboo-breaker to the young, a threatening, anti-establishment figure to their elders.

Elvis came to prominence at a time when Germany was divided into East and West, the former in the hands of the Soviet Union, the latter under the control of the Allies. The Cold War between the United States and the Soviet Union was then at its most grim and an American military presence in West Germany was deemed to be vital.

Elvis was drafted into the US Army on March 24, 1958. On October 1 he disembarked at Bremerhaven, West Germany as Army Private 53310761 to begin an eighteen-month tour with the US Third Army Division, stationed near the medieval town of Friedberg.

The presence of the controversial young rock and roll star in the heart of conservative Hesse caused an uproar. Ironically, even as West Germany was attacking Elvis for corrupting its youth, East Germany was accusing him of being a tool of anti-communist propaganda.

Caught in the middle of this bizarre black comedy, the famous young entertainer, already being haunted by secret demons of his own, gathered his family and friends around him in a rented house in the picturesque old spa town of Bad Nauheim. There he entertained a constant stream of friends, fans and lovers, practised karate, ate too much, started taking drugs, and tried with increasing desperation to maintain a private life in the full glare of his growing fame and notoriety.

Until now, very little has been known about this fascinating and sometimes tragic period in Elvis's life.

Based on the many personal interviews conducted by German fans Andreas Schröer, Michael Knorr and Oskar Hentschel, and written with the assistance of the best-selling Elvis biographer, W.A.Harbinson, *Private Presley* is the definitive record in words and rare pictures of Elvis Presley's forgotten eighteen months in Germany.

Chapter 1
EMBARKATION

US Army Private 53310761, Presley, Elvis Aaron, embarked for West Germany (now Germany) from the Military Ocean Terminal in Brooklyn, New York, on September 19, 1958. Despite the impersonal service number, the regulation haircut, and the standard issue uniform, Elvis could hardly be described as an average soldier. At twenty-three years of age, he was already the most famous young man on earth, adored and reviled in equal measure for his sensual good looks, flashy sideburns, rock and roll singing, and wild stage performances. His departure for Germany was, therefore, a media circus, adroitly organized by his flamboyant manager, Colonel Tom Parker.

Although loudly declaring that Elvis was to be treated as "just another soldier", the canny Colonel (an honorary title) had arranged for the presence of at least fifty photographers, even more reporters, and an Army brass band flanked by Naval top brass. There was a whole contingent of RCA's higher management, including Jean and Julian Aberbach and Freddie Bienstock from Hill and Range Songs; Elvis's producer, Steven Sholes; and, of course, hundreds of hysterical, screaming fans.

Also present was a recording crew, intent on taping Elvis's press conference, for release on what would be a remarkably successful "all talking" EP called *Elvis Sails*. This non-musical offering would be added to an already unprecedented list of successes that included nineteen million-selling singles in a row, numerous chart-topping albums, four box-office blockbusting movies, a wide range of money-spinning products, and over $1 million income per year. By taking a cut to his Army pay of $83.20 per month, Elvis was costing the United States an estimated $500,000 in taxes alone.

Since Elvis's induction into the Army on March 24 at Local Board 86, Main Street, Memphis, Tennessee, numerous "tribute" songs had been released, including *Dear 53310761* by the Three Teens, *Bye, Bye Elvis* by Gennie Harris, *All American Boy* by Bill Parsons and *Marchin' Elvis* by the Greats. Thousands of "Elvis" dog-tags, available in gold and silver plate and stamped with Elvis's name, rank, serial number, blood type (O), facsimile signature and etched-out picture

Above: *During his last week in Memphis prior to induction Elvis was often seen around town with his girlfriend Anita Wood. Here they are pictured leaving a car showroom.*

were marketed by Colonel Parker, as were the usual "Elvis" lipsticks, colognes, T-shirts, guitars, teddy bears and other novelty items.

Elvis's military service had been delayed three times before he was finally drafted in March 1958. On January 4, 1957 Elvis attended the Kennedy Veterans' Hospital on Jefferson Avenue in Memphis for a pre-induction physical. Thousands of young men had passed through this establishment prior to military service, but on this day the orderly hospital routine was thrown into disarray as Elvis pulled up outside in his Cadillac (license number 2D-33501). A former nurse, Mrs Benneth described it as " . . . an explosive atmosphere. The secretaries, the nurses and even the doctors stopped working and ran to the windows, just to have a look at Elvis!" A little over two hours later, Elvis climbed back into his car having been passed

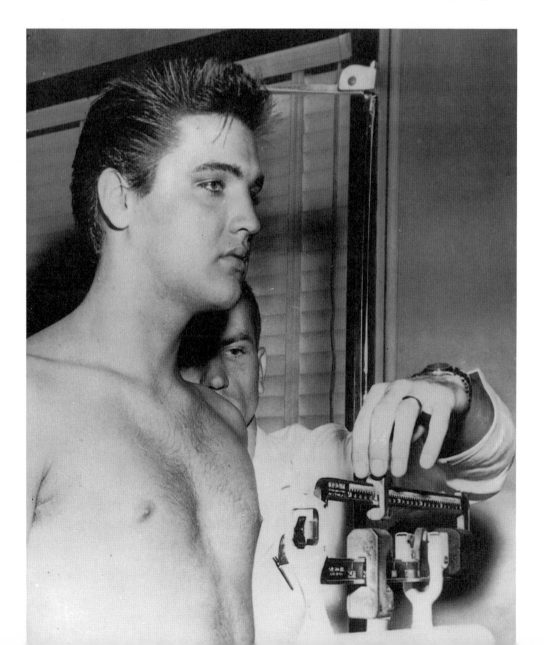

Below: *Steve Kmiec of Philadelphia adjusts the arm balance as Elvis weighs in in Memphis, March 24, 1958.*

as "A1, suitable for all military duties", but his Army days were still some way off.

The first draft order issued in January 1957 caused a storm of protest among Elvis fans and Colonel Parker managed to persuade the draft board to postpone Elvis's induction to allow him to fulfill his outstanding career commitments. This caused a backlash of protest from those who maintained that his celebrity status should not afford Elvis any preferential treatment. A second draft order came in April 1957, but this was again deferred when Colonel Parker and RCA cited contractual obligations to persuade the authorities that Elvis needed a little more time before he swapped his sequined jacket for the combat variety. Elvis was embarrassed by all the controversy his military service, or lack of it, was causing and informed reporters, "Nobody has to worry about me. I want to do my duty like every other American. My father told me, 'If you're going to be a soldier, be a good one' and that's what I intend to do."

In December 1957 Elvis finally announced that he was definitely going into the army. This caused a heated debate between Paramount and Colonel Parker. The Colonel had set up a $250,000 deal with Paramount for Elvis to star in *King Creole*. Although little work had yet been undertaken in preparations for the movie, shooting had been scheduled for January 1958. Elvis was officially drafted into the army on December 19, 1958 but the Colonel won one last sixty day deferment to allow Elvis to finish work on *King Creole*. This caused such a furor that the 83-year-old chairman of the Federal Draft Board resigned in protest. "I can't accept the responsiblity *not* to defer somebody's military service even though there are social and health reasons," he explained, "while deferring a millionaire several times." The last word on the matter, of course, went to Elvis. "Everything could have been so easy," he told friends, "if the Colonel had let me go in January '57 when Uncle Sam asked the first time."

King Creole was filmed in an incredibly short eight weeks, with Elvis walking off the set for the last time on March 22. The next day he threw a huge "Bye Bye Civilian" party at his Memphis mansion, Graceland, but he

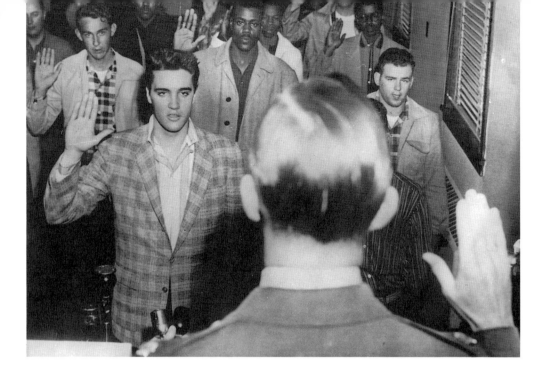

was a host with decidedly mixed emotions. He was seriously worried that his two years' absence in the Army would irreparably damage his career. Vic Morrow, one of Elvis's co-stars in the movie stated, "He's not sure if he should have named this party 'Bye Bye Business'. Well, look at this crowd and tell me - can anybody forget this guy?" At 2.30 A.M. a neighbor called the police to complain about the noise. When the police turned up at the house, Vernon Presley sent them away, assuring them that there would not be nearly so much noise during the next two years.

At 7.00 A.M. on March 24, 1958 Elvis drove his Cadillac to the Kennedy Veterans' Hospital once more. Elvis sat an IQ test conducted by Lieutenant Jack Zager and he was given a blood test before Walter Alden (father of Ginger Alden, Elvis' girlfriend at the time of his death in 1977) formally inducted him into the US Army.

Elvis was then sent to Fort Chaffee, Arkansas, where he spent four days under Sergeant Francis Johnson. He was given

Above: A tearful clutch of friends and relatives turned up to wave Elvis off as he departed for Fort Chaffee on the Army bus. These included, left to right:- Janet Hall, his aunt Vesta Presley, his cousin Patsy Presley, Anita Wood, Judy Spreckles and Bonnie Underwood.

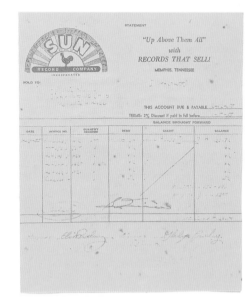

Above: *A form detailing records ELvis had ordered from Sun in 1955 countersigned by his mother as Elvis was under 21.*
Three years later Elvis was learning how to make beds and being measured up for his uniform in Fort Chaffee.

various innoculation shots, an aptitude test and a sixty-five cent haircut before being posted to Fort Hood, Texas, along with twelve other recruits including Donald (Rex) Mansfield. At Fort Hood Elvis went through eight weeks of basic combat training with A Company, Second Medium Tank Battalion, Second Armored Division, followed by eight weeks' training as an armor crewman and another six weeks of unit training under Master Sergeant Henry Coley. Most of Elvis's military activities were conducted in the full glare of publicity, again organized by Colonel Parker, cynically capitalizing on the publicity potential presented by his star's determination to do his patriotic duty.

Others were also making the most of Elvis's military service. The popular TV comedian Phil Silvers produced a thirty-minute burlesque called *Rock and Roll Rookie*, which included a song called *Brown Suede Combat Boots*; and Broadway producers Lee Adams and Charles Strouse, with writer Michael Stewart, had begun production on the musical *Bye Bye Birdie*, about the induction of a rock and roll singer named

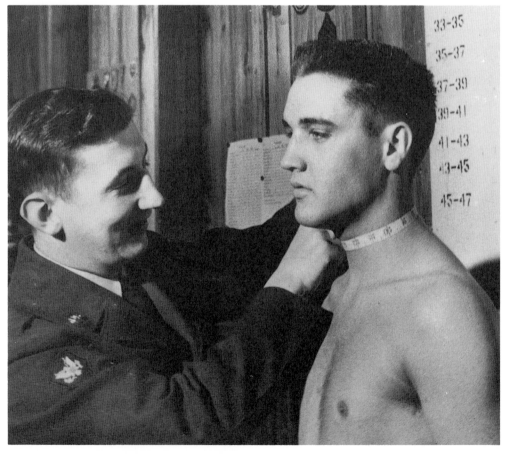

Above: *Colonel Parker kept the records coming to keep Elvis in the news*

Left: *This photograph was taken in the tailor shop at Fort Chaffee just after Elvis had had his name tag sewn on.*

Below: *Elvis gives his first salute for the camera. He told the photographer, "I'm not too good at it yet!"*

Conrad Birdie. It was then announced that in September the real Elvis (along with 1,360 other anonymous soldiers) would be sent as a replacement to the Third Armored Division in Germany. Fans wept the length and breadth of America; many protested publicly.

Despite all this success and attention, the Elvis Presley who presided over the clamorous farewell press conference at Military Ocean Terminal in Brooklyn, New York, prior to embarking for Bremerhaven, Germany, was not quite the young man he had been.

Barely three weeks before, at three o'clock in the morning of August 14, while Elvis was on compassionate leave and asleep in Graceland, his mother, Gladys Love Presley, who had been suffering from hepatitis complicated by a diet of pills and liquor, died of a heart attack.

Elvis rushed to the hospital and there, in the eloquent words of biographer Elaine Dundy, "piercing the night-time silence of the hospital and reverberating through its corridors, the wild despairing wails of Elvis and Vernon were heard as they wept and prayed, long and loud, over Gladys's lifeless body." It was a delirium of grief and pain that came close to madness.

Friends of the Presley family had always known that the relationship between Elvis and his mother was unusually close, forged in the pain of her grief over the loss of a twin brother, Jesse Garon, who died at birth, and reinforced during Vernon Presley's many absences from home. Elvis, an only child, was clearly doted upon as the survivor. If he had grown to maturity haunted by his missing "psychic twin" (his own description of Jesse Garon) he had also found compensation in his passionately adoring mother's constant attention. His mother was simply the most important person in his life.

It was also common knowledge that when Elvis became rich and famous, his only real satisfaction was in being able to ease his mother's suffering. Sadly, he was only able to

Top and above: *Elvis returns to Graceland on his first Army leave in June 1958.*

Opposite: *On compassionate leave in August 1958 with his father outside his mother's hospital room.*

do this in a material way. In trying to better her life, he not only removed her from her own world and the strength it had provided, but instilled in her the fear that she was losing him to managers, accountants, lawyers and fans. Although Elvis had sensed this, he had no way of dealing with it when Gladys died, and his anguish was compounded by the torment of guilt because he held himself responsible for her growing unhappiness and subsequent death.

The enormity of this trauma cannot be underestimated but the scenes from *Elvis - The Movie* where actor Kurt Russell, as Elvis, was seen throwing himself upon the coffin only to be forcibly dragged away, and then sobbing helplessly in his father's arms as cameras click and flashbulbs explode, are not entirely accurate. Elvis's legions of fans mourned the death of his mother and the press certainly took a morbid interest in the situation, but no photographers were present at the graveside in the Forest Hill Cemetery on August 16. The Presley family and their friends grieved alone.

With the death of his mother, Elvis went into a state of profound shock from which he would never fully emerge, although reports of him spending weeks weeping alone in his darkened bedroom are largely erroneous. In fact, the subdued and deeply distressed Private Presley was back on duty at Fort Hood just four days after the funeral. Not even the comforting normality of the military routine,

Below: *When Gladys Presley died, Elvis was practically inconsolable. Here he is pictured with his father at Graceland.*

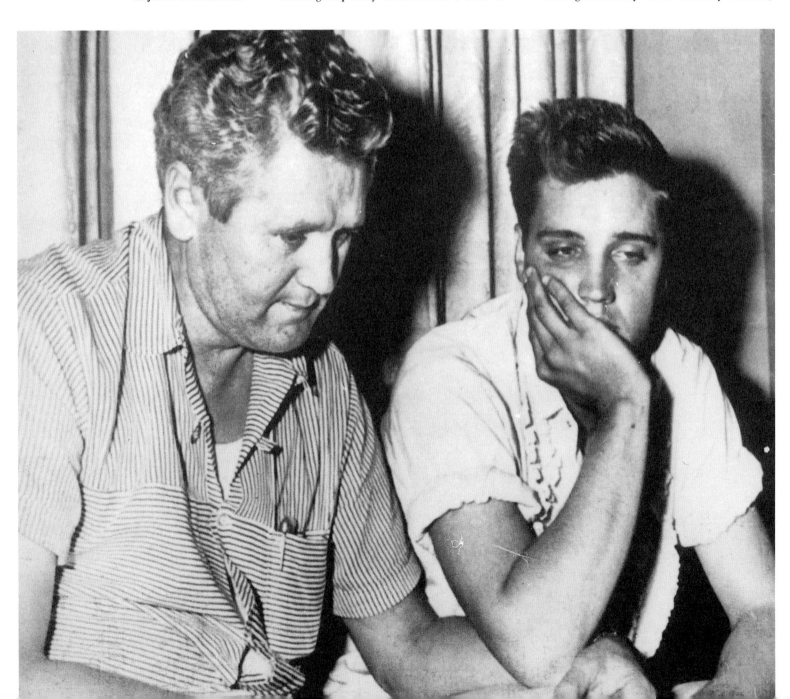

a book entitled *Poems That Touch The Heart*, marched up the gangplank of the *USS General Randall*.

Full embarkation of all the men and equipment on the massive troopship took several days and Pat Hernon managed to squeeze in one last interview with Elvis in the library of the *General Randall* shortly before the ship sailed on September 22. When asked if he had any message for his fans a quiet, almost morose Elvis revealed his fears about the future of his career. "In spite of the fact that I'm going away and that I'll be out of their eyes for some time," he said, "I hope I'm not out of their minds and I'll be looking forward to the time that I can come back and entertain again like I did."

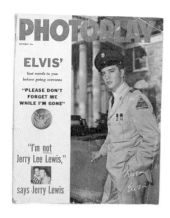

Far left: *Elvis boards the train at Fort Hood bound for Brooklyn.* Left: *The cover of* Photoplay *reflects Elvis's career worries.* Below left: *Elvis is waylaid while boarding the troopship by a persistent fan, Lillian Portnoy . . .* Below: *. . . who is rewarded with a kiss*

however, could disguise the fact that his gaze, once sleepily direct, was now focused inward.

So it was that when Elvis gave his farewell press conference at Military Ocean Terminal in Brooklyn, only a few weeks after his mother's funeral, he looked stunningly handsome in his uniform, answered the questions of the press with grace and good humor, but was otherwise disturbingly distant.

Almost everyone who had known Elvis during his adolescence and days of early fame has testified to his decency, charm and good humor. That young Elvis was still there, manifest at the press conference in Brooklyn, but another, more private, much darker Elvis was emerging.

To the accompaniment of a military band playing a medley of his rock and roll hits, Elvis shouldered his duffel bag and, carrying

Chapter 2
ARRIVAL

When Elvis disembarked at Bremerhaven on October 1, 1958, he was greeted by hundreds of cheering German fans and the same kind of media circus as the one he had left ten days ago in Brooklyn. Military police had cordoned off the whole area and blocked railway lines because there were so many fans on the tracks. Press reports about girls climbing over barbed wire fences and bursting through military police cordons were gross exaggerations. Access to the quayside at Bremerhaven was not substantially restricted and the scenes of near riot described by some newspapers occurred only in the imaginations of reporters desperate for sensational copy. The German teenagers were far more reserved than their American counterparts and had not experienced the Elvis phenomenon to anything approaching the same extent as youngsters in the US.

Above: *A young fan stands ready to greet Elvis with a cinema poster for* Loving You, *retitled in German* Gold aus heisser Kehle - *Gold From A Hot Throat.*

The arrival of Elvis was, however, an event that generated great excitement, even amongst those in the crowd who were not really Elvis fans and had come along simply to see what all the fuss was about. Newsreel cameramen and a battery of press photographers, some hoisted high above the gangplank on cranes, encouraged the more adventurous youngsters to feats of great daring. 16-year-old Karl Heinz, who confessed to never having bought an Elvis record, was persuaded to clamber up on to the gangplank to be

Left: *The USS General Randall docks at Bremerhaven, bringing Private Presley to Germany.*
Below: *Media cameramen and photographers competed for the best shots of Elvis first setting foot on German soil.*
Bottom: *Rail lines were blocked to prevent train movements because so many fans had gathered at the quayside.*

Above: Spurred on by the press corps, 16-year-old Karl Heinz almost landed the first autograph from Elvis in Germany.

photographed asking Elvis for an autograph. Awkwardly shouldering his duffel bag, Elvis tried to scrawl his signature with his free hand, failed and almost lost his balance before shaking his head and hurrying on down to the quay. A troop train was backed up all the way to the ship's disembarkation area and Elvis, along with the other bemused GIs made his way across the cleared, guarded area of passage.

One young woman, armed with desperate determination and a fragrant bouquet, had to be halted by an officer. "No flowers for Presley!" he snapped. "Soldiers don't carry

Above: *The German teen magazine BRAVO gave Elvis an enthusiastic welcome.*
Below: *The normally reserved German teenagers were also enthusiastic, but certainly not as unruly as this picture suggests. It was stage-managed by the photographers.*

flowers." The young woman was Frau Eva Windmoller, a reporter who had been given permission by RCA in Germany to interview Elvis on his arrival. The record company had given her the bouquet to present to Elvis on their behalf. She finally managed to thrust the flowers into his hand as he boarded the train and then watched as, much to her amusement, Elvis threw RCA's flowers out of the window to the crowds lining the track.

When the train pulled out of the docks, the words *Welcome to Germany, Elvis Presley* could be seen written in large, white-painted letters along the side of one of the carriages. Thus decorated, the train sped Elvis to his permanent Army post, the Friedberg Kaserne, better known as Ray Barracks, home of the 32nd ("Hell on Wheels") Battalion of the American Third Armored Division, located in the hills around Friedberg (pop.18,000), approximately two hundred miles from Bremerhaven, but only twenty miles from Frankfurt. The train arrived at approximately 7.30 in the evening, taking Elvis and his fellow GIs directly into the base.

Above: *Elvis waved goodbye to the fans and the photographers after boarding the train in Bremerhaven . . .*
Right: *. . . but the press corps was waiting for him again when he arrived at Friedberg.*

PRIVATE PRESLEY

Below: *Elvis left very little recorded material behind when he went to Germany and only three singles would be released in 1959.*

Photographers dogged his every move on his arrival at the Friedberg barracks, even photographing him lying on his barrack-room bunk.

Many of the shops in quaint old Friedberg were already filled with posters and other Elvis souvenirs in anticipation of an influx of thousands of hysterical fans. Although crowds of Elvis fans did gather outside the barracks gates, and the most dedicated of them would continue to do so throughout his stay there, stories of screaming girls overwhelming the base security to mob Elvis as he disembarked from the train are totally unfounded. At the invitation of the Army, the media, of course, were present.

Ray Barracks consisted of little more than long rows of bleak brick buildings that had once housed Hitler's SS troops and was now the unwelcoming home of the Third Armored Division. The barracks contained steel-framed beds on linoleum-covered floors, showers, latrines, a mess hall, and a PX (Post

Exchange), but not much else in the way of civilized amenities. Though more of a military post than a self-contained, fully functioning Army camp, Ray Barracks was secured behind high fences and well guarded gates.

Once safely settled in the protective embrace of the Army, Elvis was formally assigned to Company D. 1st Medium Tank Battalion, 32nd Armor, Third Army Division (battalion motto: *Victory or Death*). After drawing his field gear, including steel helmet, water bottle and size 11-D boots, from Sergeant William Patson - all the time encircled by a multitude of press reporters and photographers - Elvis was marched to bed thirteen in barracks 3707, ground floor left, where a large sack of fan mail was already waiting for him. Elvis was even photographed trying in vain to rest on his Army bed.

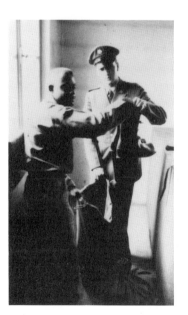

On Thursday morning, October 2, the 'ordinary' soldier attended a monster press conference in the enlisted men's canteen of the 32nd Armored Battalion, containing dozens of journalists kitted out with their own kind of battle gear, including tape-recorders, sound cameras, and notebooks. "The conference was a shade smaller than President Eisenhower might expect," a reporter noted.

For the benefit of the press, Ray Barracks had been scrupulously prepared by cleaning squads and painters who had, among other things, painted the window frames. When Elvis, prior to taking on the press corps, leant against one of the window frames, the sleeve of his new dress uniform jacket was coated with wet paint. Someone immediatley rushed off to find a bottle of paint remover to clean up the jacket and the paint stains were successfully removed. The pungent odor from the alcohol in the paint remover, however, lingered on. Refusing to walk into the conference smelling like he had just drunk a bottle of cheap whiskey, Elvis was promptly issued with another uniform jacket.

Ten pounds lighter than he had been before basic training, Elvis looked stunningly handsome, oddly distracted, and often bemused behind three microphones, but he answered the questions with grace and sly humor.

"Classical music is just great to go to sleep by," he said, offering a juicy quote for his millions of fans. Then, perhaps aware that the middle-aged would be paying attention,

Above: A huge press conference was organised on Elvis's arrival in Friedberg and Elvis fell foul of the painting crew when he leant against a window frame and coated his uniform jacket in fresh paint. A new jacket was swiftly issued before he had to go out and face the press.

Above: *Elvis conducted the press conference with his usual charm and (left) mixed with the reporters before (far left) receiving a telegram to let him know when his father, grandmother and friends would be arriving.*

The Army base at Friedberg was open to the press for three days after Elvis's initial press conference, giving ample opportunity for interviews and photographs.
Right: Elvis poses with the pony tail of Mary-Ellen Febbo, teenage editor of Overseas Weekly.

he grinned, shook his head in appealing self-admonishment, and continued with a deliberate show of modesty: "I'll be truthful. I'm no expert on music. I don't want to sit here and knock opera and classical music just because I don't understand it. I love mood music and Irish tenors," he added, clinching the point.

Asked if he'd had any trouble or ribbing from his fellow soldiers, Elvis insisted that he had not, that he had been treated just like any other GI, and that "they soon found out

I'm just like they are." Asked if he would be joining his fellow soldiers in friendly dice games, Elvis craftily said, "No, sir. I don't gamble. I have to be very careful what I do or say. Most people who like me are very young. I don't want to do anything to lose their respect, because then you're finished."

The conference was followed by a three-day period when the press and other media were allowed to roam freely over the post to get anything they wanted by way of photographs and interviews.

During this time it was announced that Elvis would be assigned to Headquarters Company as a jeep driver in a reconnaissance platoon - not as a tank driver as previously stated. This, the Army insisted, was a case of being awarded more responsibility, not less. It was a job given only to soldiers of "above normal capability" which, in this instance, included the ability to "work on his own, map-read and draw sketches, know tactics and recognize the enemy and enemy weapons."

Having thus proven that they were not according Elvis any special privileges, the Army, on October 5, closed the base to the press and other media.

This did little to make Private Elvis more private.

*   *   *

Elvis was often photographed with, on and in tanks, although he was actually a jeep driver.

Below: Left to right:- Vernon Presley, Rex Mansfield, Lamar Fike, Red West with Elvis and a journalist in Bad Homburg.

Elvis had already brought his father, Vernon Presley, grandmother, Minnie "Dodger" Mae, and friends Red West and Lamar Fike to Germany. The fact that none of these people was particularly worldly or experienced in foreign cultures would lead to problems over the next eighteen months.

Vernon's mother, Minnie Mae, then in her mid-sixties, had come to Germany to fulfil a death-bed promise to Gladys Presley, who had begged her always to stay with Elvis, no matter where he went. A skinny, feisty, independent woman, she was married at seventeen to the hard-drinking, philandering Jessie D. McClowell Presley, eight years her junior. In 1946, J.D. took off for Louisville, Kentucky, where he filed for divorce, claiming desertion. Though Minnae Mae contested this, J.D. was granted a divorce with no alimony. When he subsequently remarried, Minnie Mae, then in her late fifties, moved in with her son, Vernon, and daughter-in-law, Gladys Love.

Minnie Mae was present at Elvis's birth at 4.35 A.M. on January 8, 1935 in that now

famous two-room plank house in Tupelo, Mississippi. She would always be passionately devoted to him for that simple reason.

Born in Fulton, Mississippi, in 1916, Vernon Presley had inherited his father's good looks and unreliable character, growing into a quietly charming, unambitious man who drifted from one low-paid job to another, including sharecropping, truck driving and general laboring. Vernon married Gladys Love on June 17, 1933, but was not noticeably improved by contact with her much stronger character. In fact, on November 16, 1937, he was convicted of forging a check and sentenced to two years in the Parchman Penitentiary. The lobbying of the concerned citizens of Tupelo got him out after nine months, but the scars of the experience, as well as his consistent poverty, were never to leave him, making him notoriously tight-fisted and of a generally suspicious disposition.

Bob "Red" West first came into contact with Elvis at Humes High School, Memphis, Tennessee, where Elvis's combination of

tarist Scotty Moore, bass player Bill Black, drummer J.D. Fontana - and getting into scraps at the slightest provocation.

The huge Texan, Lamar Fike, was simply a fan from the early days who had wangled an introduction to Elvis after a concert, won his heart with his natural good-humor, and eventually became the "Court Jester" of Elvis's entourage. So devoted was Fike, he even tried to enlist at Local Board 86, Memphis, Tennessee, the day Elvis was formally inducted there, but he was rejected because of his weight, approximately 300 pounds. Elvis subsequently invited Fike to come to Germany with Minnie Mae, Vernon and Red West.

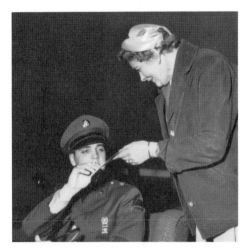

striking good looks and singing talent were gaining him the admiration of the girls and, subsequently, the antagonism of the boys. Dirt poor and ambitious like Elvis, Red had a temper to match the color of his hair. He was one of the toughest members of the school football team, and had always been quick to use his fists. One day he happened to enter the school toilet when a bunch of pupils, after catching Elvis in the act of lovingly combing his hair, were about to gang up on him. Red made them back off and thereafter he and the admiring Elvis became close friends. After graduation, Red went on to Jones Junior College on a football scholarship, helping the school win the state championship. After playing the Junior Rosebowl in Pasadena, he joined the Marines. Discharged when Elvis was on the road to fame, Red became one of Elvis's constant companions and informal bodyguard, traveling the interstates with Elvis and his original backing group - gui-

On his first 48-hour pass, Elvis visited nearby Bad Homburg with fellow GI Rex Mansfield where his father, grandmother and friends were staying in the Ritters Park Hotel. Inevitably, a journalist was present when he met them.
Above left: Elvis's strange pose is actually the method used in the Army to judge exactly where the peak of the cap should sit.

On October 6, exactly one day after the Army post was closed to the press, Elvis was enjoying his first pass with his unsophisticated family and friends in the luxurious Ritter's Park Hotel in Bad Homburg, a resort spa located a few miles from Friedberg. On October 7, Elvis moved everyone from there and into the Hilberts Park Hotel in Bad Nauheim, a beautiful old cobble-stoned town, boasting many monumental buildings, a Kurpark (a park with a spa) and numerous health clinics, where those with chest complaints and other ailments could enjoy restful holidays and the benefits of thermal baths.

A few days later, Elvis received permission to move his Army gear out of the barracks and live "off post", under the military sponsoring act, with his dependents and friends. Almost immediately, he joined them in the Hilberts Park Hotel, but they would stay there for only a brief period.

Another guest staying at the hotel at the same time as Elvis and his extended family was the oil sheik, King Ibn Saud, then one of the richest men in the world, who was there for the health treatments. Ibn Saud was constantly surrounded by his bodyguards and handed out gold watches instead of autographs. For Elvis and his entourage this first contact with truly exotic foreigners must have been highly disconcerting.

The presence of the colorfully-robed Arabs also aroused the intense curiosity of the insular, bourgeois citizens of the town, who found them far more intriguing than an American "teen" hero and his common entourage. Certainly, Elvis found the presence of the sheik and *his* entourage somewhat upsetting. The sheik attracted just as much attention from reporters and photographers as did Elvis, creating both competition and an undesirable amount of media interest in the hotel. This led Elvis to relocate his entire retinue to the Hotel Grünewald, located at 10 Terrassenstrasse, Bad Nauheim on October 11.

One of Bad Nauheim's most elegant buildings, the Grünewald has changed very little since it was first built in the nineteenth century. To this day, the hotel enjoys a preservation order which goes so far as to cover the antique furnishings, crystal chandeliers and luxurious decor, all of which must remain true to the original designs. The wealthy guests resident in

Left: *Smoking was not allowed in the Hotel Grünewald but Elvis was given special permission to smoke in his room and bought this ashtray, photographed here with his room key.*
Below: *Elvis's room key fob from the Hilberts Park Hotel*

Left: A fan profers a copy of the Elvis Presley Photo Pholio *for signature.*
Right: The signed copy.

The luxurious Hotel Grünewald in Bad Nauheim

1958 were elderly people visiting the spa town for the health cures and to enjoy a peaceful holiday. By comparison, Elvis and his brash American "family" must have seemed quite out of place and there is litle doubt that they felt ill at ease there. Red West described the Grünewald as "a sort of outpatients' hotel for heart-attack victims." His impression of the other residents was that they all "looked like they had one foot in the grave and the other one on a roller skate."

Nevertheless, Elvis rented four spacious bedrooms, all with *en suite* bathrooms, one each for himself, his father and Minnie Mae and one for Red West and Lamar Fike to share. He also rented one room on the floor below, used solely to store his bags of fan mail and, later, his secretary, Elisabeth Stefaniak.

Shortly after Elvis moved in, the ever-vigilant German press were reporting that he did not wear pajamas, but slept in his underwear, and that a Bible always lay on his night table.

The hotel generally only served break-

fast, with most guests dining out both for lunch and for an evening meal. Elvis and his entourage, however, came to an arrangement whereby, for an extra charge, they could have other meals made to order and served to them in their rooms. This meant that Elvis did not have to miss out on his favorites such as burnt bacon, fried eggs, chili without beans and weiners, or toasted peanut butter and banana sandwiches; often followed by peaches, butter and jelly or ice cream; and all washed down with milk shakes.

Red and Lamar would take care of Elvis's chores, including shining his shoes and Army boots. When they found themselves with time on their hands, they would retire to Beck's Bar, located conveniently around the corner from the hotel, where Red frequently became involved in fist fights.

Manfred Pohl, a German military policeman then attached to the US Army and now working for the US Army Public Affairs in Giessen, remembers arresting Red West after

a brawl with two policemen near the Kurhaus in Bad Nauheim. Red was held for a few hours to cool off before being released.

According to Pohl, Red fell foul of the law a second time after a bar-room quarrel with some locals. Red had been drinking and was playing the "Dollar Game" with the Germans. He would hold out a dollar bill, demonstrate how a burning cigarette end would not scorch its way through the bank-note and dare anyone to lay the bill on the back of their hand while he pressed the lighted cigarette onto it. If they could stand the heat and hold still until the note started to burn, they kept the dollar, if not, Red won himself a drink. Invariably, he won, but it was a painful experience for the loser and the fracas resulting from one such contest led to Red's arrest.

Vernon was also seen drinking heavily in the bars of Bad Nauheim and often invited everyone in the bar to join him - a form of drunken generosity that angered Elvis, as Vernon rarely carried enough cash to pay.

Top: *Behind the scenes at the Bill Haley concert in Frankfurt.*

Above: *Elvis was seldom given enough peace to stand quietly in line.*

Though in general, Elvis and his entourage liked the Germans enormously, finding them refreshingly honest, direct and good-natured, the antics of the young Americans would eventually lead to conflict with the manager of the hotel.

An early break from Bad Nauheim came on October 23 when Elvis attended a concert given in a Frankfurt cinema by Bill Haley and his Comets, the very first "white" rock and roll band and then the only serious competitor to Elvis. Haley's European tour had been disrupted by a number of riots at his concerts with seats often smashed, slashed with knives, or thrown across the auditorium. It was felt that Elvis' presence in the audience at Frankfurt could have encouraged even more hysteria and it was therefore suggested that he avoid the show and limit himself to visiting Haley in his dressing room. This he did and he also paid Haley a similar visit during the lat-

ter's Mannheim concert on the October 29.

Contrary to popular belief, though show-biz rivals at the time, Elvis and Haley were friendly. They had met before during the making of the only movie Elvis was ever to appear in as a "guest" star. Entitled *The Pied Piper of Cleveland*, the movie was produced by disc jockey Bill Randal in 1955. Randal wanted to make a film about a day in the life of a famous disc jockey and invited Elvis to Cleveland to perform a few songs for inclusion in the film. Colonel Parker agreed and they signed a contract. Unfortunately, Parker also signed a contract with 20th Century Fox for the first full-length Elvis movie, which would lead to problems.

Bill Haley and the Comets were featured in *The Pied Piper of Cleveland* as were the Four Lads and Pat Boone. Elvis sang five songs - *That's Alright, Blue Moon Of Kentucky, Good Rockin' Tonight, Mystery*

Train and *I Forget To Remember To Forget* - accompanied by Scotty Moore and Bill Black. The movie was made in color and broadcast on local TV in Cleveland in 1956. At only thirty-five minutes long it had been intended that it be shown as a "short" before the main feature when it went on general release to the cinemas. Unfortunately, the movie had been made by Universal, direct rivals to 20th Century Fox with whom Colonel Parker had signed a binding exclusive movie deal for Elvis's first films. The threat of a legal battle prevented *The Pied Piper of Cleveland* from ever being seen by the public again.

After being lost for over thirty-five years, pieces of this film have now been relocated and that which remains of the original movie is to be released on video.

Meeting Bill Haley during his visit to Germany was undoubtedly a poignant reminder to Elvis of the life he had left behind in the United States. There could be no greater contrast with the frenetic atmosphere of a rock and roll road show than that of the mausoleum-like serenity pervading the Grünewald Hotel. The ultra-conservative establishment was really no place for bored young Americans with nothing much to do and too much time in which to do it. Red West and Lamar Fike, along with Elvis when he was not at the base, burned off their excess energy by indulging their high spirits in boisterous wrestling matches, pillow fights and water pistol duels which often spilled out into the hallways.

The disturbances led to complaints from the other guests and arguments with the manager, Herr Otto Schmidt, who also suspected

Above: *Elvis playing records at home in Goethestrasse.*
Right: *Elvis with his father.*

Below: BRAVO
*magazine shows
Elvis with Cherry,
the dog he bought in
Germany.*
Bottom: *The cigar
lighter Elvis used for
his favorite
cigarillos.*

that at least one of his chambermaids was, in the words of West, "doing more to the beds in the Presley suite than just making them."

When Red and Lamar broke the bed in Elvis's room, room ten, by wrestling on it, Elvis moved temporarily into a suite upstairs. It boasted a piano, which Elvis played in the evening, often singing with his friends. The hotel's elderly guests did not appreciate these impromptu performances and lost no time in making their feelings known to Herr Schmidt. He, in turn, complained to Elvis. His tedious reprimands about the behavior of his American guests now occurred with depressing regularity, and his patience was wearing thin.

To make matters worse, on November 28, Elvis bought a dog named Cherry, which he then couldn't look after because he was working at the base all day. Herr Schmidt was later to complain that the girl in his kitchen, or sometimes he personally, looked after the dog more than Elvis's family or friends did. This can have done little to improve relations between them.

Things came to a head when Elvis locked himself into his room during a shaving-cream fight and Red tried to smoke him out by

putting paper under the door and then setting fire to it. When the smoke drifted out into the hallway, many of the elderly residents thought the building was on fire and the manager ordered the Presley party to leave.

Consequently, in late December, after returning from maneuvers in Grafenwöhr, Elvis started looking for a house to rent. This was not to be an easy undertaking. Red West and Lamar Fike roamed the streets of Bad Nauheim, knocking on doors and asking if the owners wanted to rent. The problem was that the locals of the staid old spa town were not keen to have a rock and roll star in their homes. Some thought it was a joke. Others had heard stories about how Elvis and his clan had been forced to leave two hotels because of their wild behavior. At 14 Goethestrasse, however, the shrewd Frau Pieper realized that renting to the rich Americans would provide her with a handsome income. She said "Yes" to the foreigners.

Though rumors had been circulating that Elvis and his father had been looking for a castle or medieval mansion, they certainly didn't move into one. Because he was famous, Elvis was compelled to pay over one thousand

Deutschmarks (then around $800), per month - about four or five times the going rate - to owner Frau Pieper, for the privilege of living in 14 Goethestrasse.

The house certainly did not warrant that kind of rental. It was a modest three-storied, four-bedroom, white-painted building in poor state of repair. In addition, Frau Pieper insisted on remaining in the house, moving into an attic bedroom and sharing the kitchen with the exasperated Minnie Mae. The main entrance to the house was through a side door which led into a small vestibule where there was space to hang coats. A frosted glass door led into the main living area. This modestly furnished room ran the whole length of the front of the building with doors leading off to the kitchen and bathroom at the back of the house. In the far corner of the room stood the piano around which Elvis and the others would gather in the evening. A staircase led to an upper hallway and the four bedrooms, with Elvis and Vernon occupying the two at the back of the house and Minnie Mae one of the front rooms, while Red and Lamar shared the other. The staircase then continued up to Frau Pieper's attic room.

Life at 14 Goethestrasse was something of a cabaret. In January 1959, Elvis had rented the piano for forty Deutschmarks per month from the Kuehlwetter music shop. He was to play it frequently during the rest of his stay in Frau Pieper's house. He played mainly in the evenings when, far from annoying his neighbors as some reports would have it, the shutters on the living room windows would be closed not just to keep the noise in, but to discourage passers by from calling for requests. Minnie Mae also accompanied herself on the piano while singing country and western songs and Elvis always responded with an encouraging, "Very good, Omi!"

One thing Minnie Mae and Frau Pieper

had in common was their fondness for alcohol. Minnie Mae loved miniatures, which she could hide in her pockets since Elvis, a non-drinker, did not approve. Minnie Mae and Frau Pieper were often seen together having coffee and cognac in the local cafes. Drinking was a habit Minnie Mae shared with her son, Vernon, and his former wife, Gladys.

Minnie Mae's relationship with Frau Pieper was a mixture of antagonism and affection: They fought over the kitchen, the running of the house, and the rowdy behavior of Elvis and his friends. The relationship, however, was also one of guarded mutual affection based on lengthy conversations in which neither woman fully understood what

Top: *14 Goethestrasse then and now.*
Middle: *Minnie Mae Presley with Frau Pieper.*
This photo was taken by Elvis and hand tinted.
Above: *Elvis at home in Goethestrasse.*

Right: Baker Walter Knasmöller treated Elvis to several of his special cakes and went on to become a master chef running a successful business in Germany.

the other was saying. Once, when they were drinking together, Minnie Mae was seen to be crying. Frau Pieper couldn't understand what Minnie Mae was saying, but was in no doubt that she was pouring her heart out over Vernon's secret, burgeoning affair with a mysterious blonde lady.

Minnie Mae did not go out often, making the house her kingdom, although she sometimes went shopping with Frau Pieper, to buy food for Elvis. He especially loved chili con carne without beans, so she bought the meat and the other ingredients. When Frau Pieper couldn't go with her, she would give Minnie Mae a list in German. Most of the other food - bacon, bananas, peanut butter, ice cream - was bought in the local shops, but what couldn't be found there was purchased from the PX by Vernon.

Minnie Mae prepared the food for Elvis and the family, trying to learn German dishes, particularly chocolate cake. Frau Pieper tried to explain various recipes, but this only caused more friction between them, particularly when Frau Pieper tasted the food with her finger. They argued over how food should be cooked, they argued over how it should be prepared, and they argued over the organization of the kitchen - all without the benefit of common language. There was so much friction, in fact, that Minnie Mae once attacked Frau Pieper with a broom.

Frau Pieper refused to spend money on the maintenance of the house, so it was not in very good condition. What particularly irked Elvis and his entourage was the state of the garden. When they played badminton there, which they did a lot, they often lost the shuttlecock because the grass was so long. Eventually, on July 7, Elvis drove to Friedberg in his white BMW, parked his car on the main street, and went into the gardening shop, Samen Herman, where he purchased a lawnmower for 289 Deutschmarks - a very expensive item of the time. Next day, he gave the lawnmower to Frau Pieper, hinting that she should mow the lawn. She didn't. Thereafter Red West or Lamar Fike were the ones seen using Frau Pieper's unwanted present.

Frau Pieper knew Elvis was rich and that it was good to have him in the house, but the incident with the lawnmower demonstrates her apparent attitude of indifference towards this lucrative arrangement. Well aware of the problems Elvis had encountered while searching for a house to rent, and exploiting a situation which was working totally to her advantage, she was quite happy to sit back and let the money roll in. Indeed, she even made some extra cash by selling off many of Elvis's personal belongings, particularly clothes, to visiting fans right up to the day he left for home.

Above: *Young girls were an ever-present feature outside Elvis's house. Some were very young indeed.*

Right: *Another baby is offered for cradling in Elvis's arms, this time at the waste ground near his house where he was playing football.*
Below: *The shirt Elvis wore to play football that day.*
Below right: *Receipt and guarantee for the lawnmower Elvis bought in Friedberg.*

do just that (this may account for the erroneous reports about Vernon) and he and Lamar had a bad reputation as ill-mannered foreigners. They often drank in the bar of a hotel on Terrassenstrasse. The main reason for the trouble was still that Red and Lamar, who rarely received money from Elvis, would drink all night and then say they would pay the next day. As the people in the local bars were not impressed by Red and Lamar's friendship with Elvis, tempers would become frayed and Red would strike out, starting another brawl.

Lamar Fike was called "Buddha" by Elvis and "the Fat one" by the German locals and press. Though no more sophisticated than Red, when alone he was much nicer - and particularly good to the fans who gathered outside in Goethestrasse. Red West, on the other hand, often treated the fans with contempt.

One of the many visitors to the house was Rex Mansfield, who had been inducted with Elvis at Memphis and who came to Germany with him on the *USS General Randall*. Rex was genuinely fond of Elvis and would soon be practising karate with him, but he learned early on that the sure way to lose Elvis's friendship was to talk about him to the press. Another friend from basic training at Fort Hood was Donald Pettit, who had bunked with Elvis in the same cabin on the *General Randall*. Unfortunately, Pettit made the mistake of writing a story called "Elvis in the

Vernon, who had started drinking a lot after Gladys died, was even more heavily into it in Germany. Though many of the locals were aware of Vernon's heavy drinking, an anonymous reporter on the German newspaper *Bild am Sonntag* went so far as to state that "one used to see Vernon with a scratched face and black eyes, which he must have received after fights in bars in Frankfurt."

While Vernon undoubtedly drank, it is unlikely that he actually fought in bars. Red West on the other hand continued to

Army" for a special release magazine, which included photos of Elvis with Pettit and his family. When Elvis saw the article, he cut Pettit dead, never letting him into the group again, let alone into 14 Goethestrasse.

Privacy was important to Elvis, given what he went through with the fans. For this reason, even his private dentist, Dr Atta, in Bad Nauheim, would open in the evening especially for him, as did his hairdresser, Herr Leutzer, of the Salon Jean Hemer. Elvis also acquired his own local taxi-driver, Joseph Wehrheim, who had once been the personal driver of American newspaper magnate, William Hearst. Elvis used him not only as a chauffeur, but as a well-paid messenger boy, sent out for everything from chocolate bars to chewing gum.

When Gladys Presley was alive Elvis had led a reasonably open, natural life, but after she died and as his celebrity status in America grew, it became impossible for him to walk down the street or call into a record store without being mobbed. The barriers he had started to build around him in the United States were partially relaxed in Bad Nauheim. Once the initial novelty of having a famous rock and roll star in their midst had worn off, Elvis was able to move quite freely through the streets of the old town, having to contend with only the occasional nervous teenage autograph hunter. In short, he found Bad Nauheim refreshingly relaxing, although fans continued to gather outside his house there.

The best way to prove you'd been close to Elvis was to be photographed with him outside his house. The next best thing was to pose with his famous BMW decorated with records.

Elvis grew more fond of the Germans as he settled into his new surroundings. Initially he enjoyed himself with the local youths. He engaged in friendly firework fights with them, and either wrestled or played football with them together with his fellow GIs on the waste ground near his house.

Unfortunately, when word spread beyond the town that Elvis was living in Goethestrasse, the fans came from far and wide to keep vigil outside the house, hoping to catch sight of their idol and pick up an autograph. This forced him into a more reclusive existence.

If Elvis wanted to go out without having to brush off the star-struck autograph hunters, Lamar Fike would drive the car around the back of the house, and Elvis would climb over the garden fence. Eventually, it

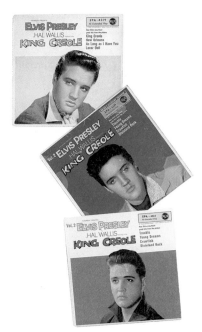

41

was deemed necessary to put a sign on the door, stating "Autographs between seven-thirty and eight-thirty P.M." Elvis travelled to and from the post at Friedberg either in his second-hand black Mercedes, sometimes driven by Lamar Fike, or in his recently purchased white BMW. In stark contrast to the situation at home in Goethestrasse, where Elvis was surrounded by constant reminders of his celebrity status, at the army base he was treated like any other GI.

Rising early in order to breakfast and have an unhurried twenty to thirty minute drive to Friedberg, Elvis would be at the base by 7.00 A.M. There, he would help "police" the area, which meant picking up every piece of windblown trash or, in his own words, "Everything not nailed to the ground." At 7.40 A.M. he was on parade for drill call, which often lasted an hour. Invariably this was followed by a physical training session, then early morning inspection of the barracks. After an hour of "Motor Stables", that was cleaning and maintaining his jeep, he

would have a busy day of map reading, scouting, patrolling, and driving his platoon sergeant, Master Sergeant Ira Jones, from Missouri, wherever he needed to go. While it is true that he returned home for lunch, this was really only because he couldn't have any peace in the chow line, where the other GIs would be constantly staring at him, wanting to talk to him. Apart from that break, Elvis put in as long and hard a day as anyone else in the regiment. By six in the evening, he was home for supper. At 7.30 P.M. he would go outside, usually still in his Army fatigues and cap, to sign autographs for the patiently-waiting fans. He would chat as best he could, knowing very little German, and it was not unusual for him to spend more than two hours at his own front gate.

At work, Elvis didn't have it any easier than any other GI and in certain areas, he had it worse. His Army duties were often carefully choreographed by the Army public relations men to ensure that there were reporters and photographers on hand for

maximum publicity. Unfortunately, stories about Elvis carrying out humdrum tasks like any other soldier do not make exciting copy and reporters often spiced up their stories with wild accounts of girls trying to break into the base, wriggling under barbed wire fences to try to get at Elvis. The truth is that security at the base was too tight for any such adventures. This was, after all, the height of the Cold War. Manfred Pohl, whose duties as a military policeman would have included controlling unruly fans, states quite clearly that: "There were often girls waiting at the gate to try to catch a glimpse of Presley, but they never caused any trouble. The only time we were ever called out to a disturbance reportedly involving Elvis fans was when the street outside his hotel was blocked but this turned out not to be rioting Elvis fans but angry motorists stuck in a traffic jam on their way to an ice hockey game at a stadium near where Presley was staying."

Sometimes there were more problems with Elvis's Army colleagues than there were with the fans. Troops from other units were offered a fifty dollar reward and a thirty-day pass if they captured Elvis when on maneuvers. But according to his platoon sergeant, Ira Jones, Elvis "scrubbed, washed, greased, painted, marched, ran, carried his laundry and worried through inspections just as everyone else did."

Elvis's life was made no easier by the fact that others were harassing him in a different way. German disc jockey Wernher Goetze had repeated an American DJ's stunt of breaking Elvis's records on the air and had complained that Elvis was corrupting German youth "away from their lederhosen for blue jeans." Not to be outdone, a noted German archaeologist, Ferdinand Anton, stated on the Armed Forces Radio Network that Elvis was "a throwback to the Stone Age." This did not pre-

vent thousands of fans from jamming the base switchboard lines with outraged calls from all over the world. Nor did it effect the massive amount of fan mail Elvis received. As many as ten thousand letters a week were flooding in, many addressed only to "Elvis, US Army", some to "Colonel" or "General" Presley. The letters were sent on to Elvis via Colonel Parker's office in Madison, Tennessee.

There, apart from supervising the answering of Elvis's voluminous mail, and despite the diminishing number of recordings in the vaults, the Colonel was battling to keep his "boy" in the public eye. Recent releases had included the EP soundtracks from *Love Me Tender* and *Jailhouse Rock*, plus the *Loving You* and *King Creole* soundtrack albums, all of which were hot sellers. There was, however, a distinct lack of new material. Although two EPs of material from *King Creole* would remain high in the charts for most of 1959, there were only enough new recordings for three more singles: *A Fool Such As I/I Need Your Love Tonight*; *One Night/I Got Stung*; and *A Big Hunk O'Love/My Wish Came True*. RCA was frantic for new product and begged the Colonel to let Elvis cut some records in Germany. The Colonel resolutely refused, insisting that his boy perform only his military duty. He did, however, make up for the lack of new records by supervising the February release of *For LP Fans Only*, an album of previously released singles, some five years old.

Chapter 3
OUT ON MANEUVERS

On November 3, 1958, during his second month in Germany, Elvis joined the 32nd Tank Battalion in Friedberg, as part of Combat Command C of the Third Army Division, on special training maneuvers in the area of Grafenwöhr, a hellishly cold, snow-covered area of wooded hills not far from the border of then Communist Czechoslovakia. During the exercises, he practised his map reading, rifle marksmanship and observation of enemy positions while suffering the freezing cold and primitive living conditions. In the words of Lieutenant-General F.W. Farrell, the commanding officer of V Corps: "Presley was cold, wet and ankle-deep in snow, just like everyone else."

Not quite. In fact, Elvis's first maneuvers gave the Army a considerable headache. As the PR potential of the exercises could not be discounted, reporters were told they could come along. It was soon realized, however, that no-one was interested in watching the Army at work, but only in following Private Presley when he went off to practise with his Army 45 Automatic pistol, his M1 rifle, his jeep's 30-and-50 Calibre machine-guns, and the 90mm guns of the M48 tanks.

The maneuvers had barely begun when the training area was declared out-of-bounds

With the press out in force and a "price on his head", much of the maneuvering took place round Elvis.

44

to the press. This, of course, did not prevent the reporters from flocking to the district. Again the press were frustrated by an exasperating lack of sensational copy and again stories began to circulate about the ruthless, cunning Elvis fans, this time infiltrating the strict security around the training area in some bizarre maneuvers of their own, slithering along ditches in the hope of catching sight of their hero.

The situation was even more exasperating for the Army which found that it was having problems with its own officers, many of whom were pulling rank or even *using* the maneuvers in order to make contact with Elvis. They would beg him to perform at their battalion functions, sign autographs for their wives, children and friends, or come visit when the maneuvers were over for some home cooking and real Southern hospitality.

Most of the maneuvering, then, almost certainly took place around Elvis. The rest was a farce.

In 1945, at the end of World War II, the defeated Nazi Germany was divided into four occupation zones by the US, Britain, France, and the USSR. In 1949 the three western zones became the Federal German Republic (West Germany), the eastern zone became the German Democratic Republic (East Germany), and Berlin, the former capital, was divided into East Berlin and West Berlin. Eventually the political "Iron Curtain" dividing the former Germany was given concrete form by the Soviets in the building of their infamous Berlin Wall.

Those events, and the growing antagonism between East and West, ensured the continuing presence of British, French and American troops in West Germany. By 1958, when Elvis arrived in West Germany as one of those troops, the so-called "Cold War" between the Soviet Union and the United States was at its height and Elvis became a convenient tool in the propaganda war between them.

For this reason, his presence near the border inspired a virulent "anti-Elvis" campaign from the Communists, with *Neues Deutschland* describing him as a "Cold War Weapon" and "an advertisement for NATO in the West Zone." Another East German paper, *Young World*, accused him of being a tool of "those persons plotting an atomic war" - an accusation rationalized with the paper's

Above: *As in Friedberg, Elvis's celebrity status did not afford him any special privileges. He had to get his hands dirty like everyone else.*

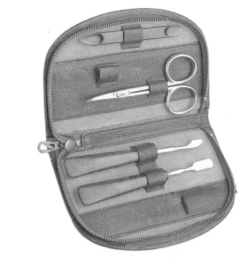

Above: *Elvis didn't mind getting his hands dirty, but this monogramed manicure set meant they didn't have to stay that way!*

insistence that "youths dumb enough to become Presley fans are dumb enough to fight in a war."

While the Soviet youth newspapers, *Komsomolskaya Pravda* and *Moskovsky Komsomolets*, were taking turns accusing Elvis of being part of the West's "ideological battle" to subvert Communist youth, the leader of a juvenile gang in Halle, East Germany, was arrested for buying Elvis records and hanging a signed picture of the subversive rock and roll singer in his living room. In Leipzig, the members of another juvenile gang, the Elvis Presley Hound Dogs, were arrested for falling under the influence

of "NATO ideology" and committing anti-state acts by performing Elvis Presley songs.

Encouraged by this, State Department officials in the US tried to persuade Elvis to perform for the troops and perhaps do a little propaganda work, but Elvis, or Colonel Parker, refused. This refusal to place Elvis in the Army's Special Services branch or for him to act as an advertisement for the Army had been steadfast since even before his induction.

The determination not to let Elvis be anything other than just an "ordinary soldier" has long been viewed as one of the Colonel's masterstrokes, enabling him to state

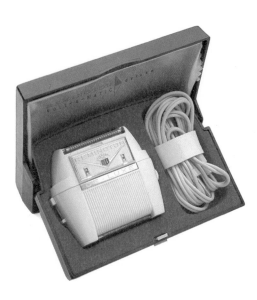

Right: *Elvis using the shaver pictured above. It was a pesent from his father. Vernon had an identical one.*

repeatedly that his "boy" didn't want any "special treatment" or "the easy way out", but instead would do his duty like every other humble GI. But, while the Colonel was certainly responsible for the cynical exploitation of Elvis's army service, Elvis himself was proud of his achievements and promotions in the Army, wanted very much to be respected as a "normal" GI, and would have been a good soldier with, or without, the Colonel's encouragement.

In refusing to perform while in the Army, Elvis put himself under immense pressure, most of it coming from senior officers who wanted him to sing in public or private; but it certainly worked for him in the long run, winning the hearts of those parents who had previously discouraged their children from following in the footsteps of the outrageous Pied Piper of rock and roll. Now, in serving his country with dignity and distinction, Elvis was seen as being part of the very establishment he had previously threatened.

"He doesn't want to entertain," Major General Thomas F. Van Natta, commanding officer of the 3rd Armored Division, finally conceded. "We've asked him and he said, 'I'd rather not, sir.' I think he feels he has an obligation to his country and he wants to pay it like everyone else and get it over with… He's a good soldier."

While in Grafenwöhr, Elvis met the nineteen-year-old Elisabeth Claudia Stefaniak, whose German father had been reported "missing" during the war, only to turn up years later with a Russian wife. After an acrimonious divorce, Elisabeth's mother had married an American Army sergeant, Raymond McCormick, also stationed in Grafenwöhr. Forbidden by her stepfather to date any GIs and unable to get a job because, although

German-born to a German mother, technically she was an American, Elisabeth was leading a dismal life when she met Elvis Presley.

Another GI, Johnny Lange, who joined Elvis and Rex Mansfield two or three times a week at the local cinema, the Post Theatre, indirectly introduced Elisabeth to Elvis. This was no accident. In fact, Elisabeth had read about Elvis's arrival in Grafenwöhr in the *Stars & Stripes* newspaper and, as a genuine Elvis fan, decided to waylay him at the cinema and try for his autograph.

At first she had problems because Elvis and his friends always arrived at the cinema ten minutes late and left a few minutes before the end of the show to avoid causing a stir. Eventually she spotted him in the audience with Rex Mansfield and Johnny Lange. When Lange got up to purchase some popcorn, Elisabeth gave him a piece of paper and begged him to ask Elvis for his autograph. Lange agreed to do so (Elisabeth was very pretty), but when he returned to his seat and whispered a few words to Elvis, Rex Mansfield

Below: *Escape and evasion may have been on the maneuvers agenda but there was no escaping or evading press men hunting autographs!*

Elisabeth's six-year-old sister, Linda, that Elvis had arrived and little Linda, not recognizing Elvis, had refused to let him in as her father was sleeping. A kindly neighbor, having overheard the doorstep exchange, invited Elvis to wait in his house instead.

When visiting the family, Elvis often played guitar and sang for them. He also talked a lot about his family, particularly his mother, revealing that he still missed her desperately, often crying when he mentioned her name. His strong family ties were also emphasized by the fact that he phoned his father back in Bad Nauheim every day.

Apart from the Post Theatre, there were few places Elvis could take Elisabeth for privacy, other than to go for drives in a car borrowed from her stepfather. At first, Elisabeth found it exciting to have crowds of fans (mainly the children of other servicemen housed in family accommodation on the base) constantly gathered in front of her home, but

got up, approached Elisabeth, and told her that Elvis wanted her to sit beside him.

Completely captivated, Elisabeth thought that Elvis, up close, was "the most handsome, most beautiful hunk of man I had ever seen." This explains why she did not resist when he boldly put his arm around her and asked her name. Elisabeth would never remember the rest of that first conversation - only that Elvis walked her home after the show and kissed her goodnight.

Soon, Elisabeth and Elvis were seeing each other three or four times a week, mostly to go to the movies and enjoy the ten-minute walk home. Elvis then started dropping into the McCormick house on a regular basis, charming her parents with his customary ease. Elisabeth recalls that the first time he dropped in, unexpectedly, she was out with her mother. Arriving home, they found about twenty-five kids gathered outside the house. Slipping inside, they learnt from

eventually they became a problem as they were watching the house constantly and ringing the doorbell almost every five minutes, begging Elvis to come out and sign autographs.

On November 27, Elvis was promoted to Private First Class (PFC), receiving his first stripe from his commander, Capt. Edward E. Betts, and a salary raise to $99.37 per month.

On December 20, the day of his return to Friedberg, he dropped in on Elisabeth and her parents, to say goodbye. During the course of this visit he informed them that he needed a secretary back in Bad Nauheim, to act as interpreter and deal with his many bags of fan mail. He offered Elisabeth the job. Her parents agreed and soon their daughter was on her way to Bad Nauheim, to live with Elvis, his father, his grandmother, Red West and Lamar Fike.

Initially Elisabeth stayed in a room in the Hotel Grünewald, where Elvis and his entourage were still in residence, but later she moved with them to 14 Goethestrasse.

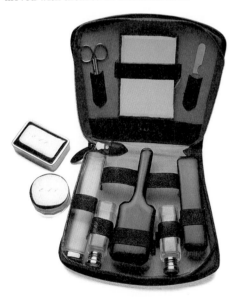

As Elvis's secretary, Elisabeth Stefaniak was kept very busy. Most of her work consisted of dealing with the huge amounts of fan mail, and she certainly found the letters intriguing. Some were covering notes for gifts, many were requests for autographed pictures; there were a lot of love letters and hate letters from jealous boyfriends or husbands; and quite a few were from people wanting money. In dealing with this mail, Elisabeth was helped by Red

Above: *This monogramed vanity set helped keep Elvis well groomed in the wilds of Grafenwöhr.*

and Lamar, both of whom could expertly forge Elvis's signature.

"She was like a pet to him," an unnamed friend informed biographer Jerry Hopkins about Elisabeth. "He delighted in her naïveté and responses to his generosity. He mentioned bringing her to America with him if her father approved. Her father did not approve."

In fact, the exact nature of this relationship is still not clear, though Rex Mansfield, a frequent visitor to the house who later married Elisabeth, suggests that "she was a lot more to him than a secretary."

This seems to have been true. Certainly, Elisabeth's own recollections suggest she was one of Elvis's girlfriends at the time. Elizabeth confesses that she "resented any girl coming" and that when Janie Wilbanks arrived to spend a holiday in the Hotel Grünewald, she "became very jealous" at first. (Wilbanks was famous-for-a-day after being photographed kissing Elvis through the window of the train in Memphis.) Within days, Elisabeth became friends with Wilbanks, though the friendship certainly surprised her: "After all, she was my competition." Gradually, Elisabeth was forced to accept that she and Janie Wilbanks were "only two peas in a big pod full of girls" and that she would have to learn to share Elvis with the others.

Elisabeth also learned soon enough that Elvis would not allow any of his girls even to look at another man - and would positively explode if a man looked at them. Despite this, Red West, an inveterate womanizer who used his friendship with Elvis to bait the girls, would often arrive drunk from Beck's Bar and come into Elisabeth's room "to just talk." Knowing how Elvis felt about such matters, this always made Elisabeth very nervous.

As Elisabeth also discovered, Elvis could be hot-tempered for other, more minor reasons. For instance, on one of the rare occasions when he went shopping with her alone, without the bodyguards, and was about to buy a trash can for his room, Elisabeth made the mistake of simply reminding him

Right: *Looking ghostly white in the bitterly cold forest area, Elvis is captured by another lurking photographer.*

Left: *The Army had no height restriction for its recruits but this one probably lied about his age.*
Below: *Elvis chatting with sergeant Johnny Mathis.*

that he already had one. Burning her up with his gaze, Elvis said, "Don't you ever tell me what or what not to buy. If I want a thousand trash cans in my bedroom, that's my business." He then stormed from the store without completing his purchase. When Elisabeth apologized, hardly knowing why she was doing so, he added insult to injury by telling her that he had planned to buy her some new clothes, but she "had ruined it." He didn't speak to her for days... and the offer to buy her new clothes was never repeated.

On the whole, however, life was fun with Elvis - even more so when he moved out of the Grünewald and into the house at 14 Goethestrasse. There, he was often visited by GI friends, including Rex Mansfield and Charlie Hodge. As both Hodge and Red West could sing and play the guitar, they often joined Elvis in song around the piano in the living room.

Chapter 4
PUBLIC RELATIONS AND PRIVATE DRAMAS

Left: *Elvis with his Volkswagen*
Right: *The press made much of Elvis's glamorous new car.*
Below: *Elvis was presented with his car keys by German game show hostess Uschi Siebert.*

Elvis's first car in Germany was an old Volkswagen which he eventually gave to his German karate instructor, Jürgen Seydel. The car was in poor condition and Seydel left it outside his house as a bizarre garden ornament where it remains to this day. Elvis also owned a Mercedes saloon but his personal transport was to be something more exotic.

Returning to Friedberg from Grafenwöhr, on December 20, 1958, Elvis was awarded a three-day pass for excelling on maneuvers. He celebrated by purchasing a demonstration model white BMW 507 sports car. Upholstered in white leather and previously used by the famous German racing driver, Hans Stuck, it was one of only two hundred and fifty three ever built. The purchase was arranged as a promotional ploy by the Bavarian Motor Works of Munich, through BMW Gloceckle, Frankfurt, who offered him the $7,160 vehicle at the greatly reduced price of $3,750. The press was present at the showroom, waiting to photograph Elvis being presented with the keys to his car by Frau Uschi Siebert, a former beauty queen and TV game-show hostess.

Elvis was later to discover that the contract he had signed, which was written in German and incomprehensible to him, was not for the purchase of the car at all, but a leasing agreement. The BMW dealer would ask for the return of the car when Elvis was preparing for his return to America. The situation was further complicated by the fact that Elvis had the car painted red in August 1959, partly to alleviate the problem of fans scrawling messages in lipstick on the bodywork. BMW were furious that he had changed the color without consulting them and when the

Below: Anxious not to be left out of the proceedings, the owner of the BMW dealership also presented Elvis with the keys.
Right: Elvis didn't take delivery of the car on the day of the presentation, but he did go for a spin to provide further photo opportunities.

Left: Elvis signed a contract he did not fully understand.

Left: *German racing driver Hans Stuck had raced the car in several sports car events, but the engine was modified for Elvis to use the car on a daily basis.*
Below: *Elvis was also reported to have bought a BMW Isetta "bubble car" but actually only posed with this car for publicity shots.*

Below: *Vernon also tried out the car for size.*
Bottom: *To the annoyance of the press, Elvis took time out from their photo call to talk to some children.*

Elvis's official 1958 Christmas card.

car was returned to them, they repainted it in the original white, presenting Elvis with the bill which he refused to pay. The car is still in existence today and has had many celebrity owners since Elvis, including the German actor Kurt Jurgens, and it is even more of an expensive and desirable machine now than it was in the fifties. It makes regular appearances at classic car shows in Germany although the owner is reluctant to admit that his car was once owned by Elvis for fear of losing his wing mirrors to a souvenir-hunting fan. Ironically, he has changed the color of the car back to red again.

On the day Elvis was presented with the car, he did not drive the BMW away. Instead, Vernon drove him, along with Red

and Lamar, back to Bad Nauheim in the black Mercedes, with Elvis beside him and the others in the back. On the way home, they were hotly pursued by a photographer in another car. In an attempt to shake him off, Vernon accelerated through a railroad crossing just as the gates were coming down. Unable to make it past the far gate before it was lowered, the Mercedes and its occupants were trapped between it and the track just as the train was about to pass through. By slewing the Mercedes sideways, Vernon managed to maneuver the car far enough away from the track for it to be left unscathed when the train roared past. Then, when the barriers were lifted, he was able to take off and elude the reporter.

Unfortunately, this was not the only "near miss" by the notoriously careless Vernon. On January 1, 1959, only eleven days after the dangerous railroad crossing incident, Elvis reportedly "died" in an accident after crashing his black Mercedes.

In fact, the accident occurred when Vernon was driving Elisabeth Stefaniak back to Bad Nauheim after a shopping trip to the PX and commisary at Frankfurt. On the Frankfurt-Kassel autobahn, Vernon accelerated to pass the car in front of him just as that car also started pulling out. Vernon then hit the brakes too hard, causing the Mercedes to go into a skid, roll over a few times, and fly across the oncoming lanes, finally crashing into a tree at the far side of the autobahn.

The Mercedes was a terrible mess, a total write-off, with the groceries, including broken eggs, spilled all over the rear seats.

Above: *A close call for Elvis, Red and Lamar when Vernon maneuvered them into trouble on a rail crossing.*

On December 26, 1958, Elvis visited the "Holiday On Ice" show in Frankfurt. As the audience profile was somewhat different to that of a rock and roll concert, it was thought safe enough for Elvis to enjoy the show from among the crowd.

Above: *Elvis with one of the skaters*
Top left and left: *Red West's broad shoulders were put to good use when it came to signing autographs backstage.*

As most of the ice dancers were English or American, Elvis was able to enjoy himself chatting with them and an irresistable photo opportunity presented itself when he helped one of them lace up her boots.

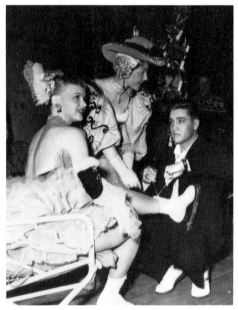

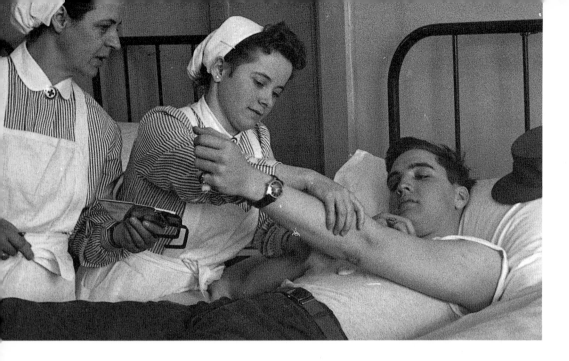

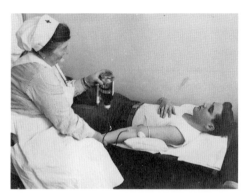

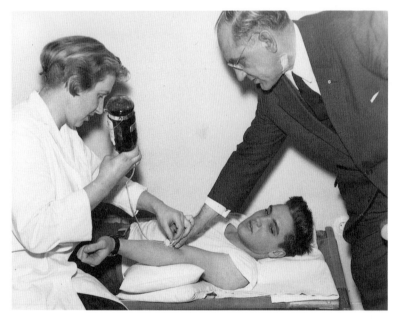

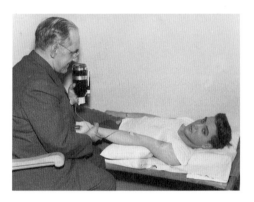

Vernon had a few bruises, but was otherwise unhurt. Elisabeth, on the other hand, did not get off so lightly. Temporarily paralyzed and thinking she had broken her back, she was rushed to hospital by ambulance while Vernon remained with the wrecked car.

X-rays taken at the hospital revealed that Elisabeth was badly bruised but had no broken bones. Her temporary paralysis, already gone, had been caused by shock. She looked worse than she actually felt because her head had been cut in several places by broken glass.

Elvis was in 14 Goethestrasse when a motorist who had stopped at the scene of the accident rang Frau Pieper at Vernon's request. Receiving only a garbled version of events from Frau Pieper, Elvis drove with Red and Lamar to the accident scene, fearing he had now lost his father, as well as his mother. Arriving there, he was shocked by the condition of the car and he was convinced that his father had perished in the accident. Vernon, meanwhile, had made his way back to Goethestrasse and missed Elvis en route.

Elvis rushed to see Elisabeth in the hospital where, doubtless also in a state of shock, he forgot to ask how she was feeling and instead practically accused her of having caused the accident by having a secret affair with his father. It was then that Elisabeth first realised that Elvis, who appeared to have the world at his feet, "was suspicious of everyone around him, even including his own Dad."

Meanwhile, local reporters had picked up the story of the accident and were wiring sensational stories about it, claiming that Elvis was seriously injured, perhaps even dead. After reading such reports, fans in the

United States and elsewhere were profoundly shocked. Within hours, they had placed more than 200,000 advance orders for his forthcoming RCA single: *One Night/I Got Stung*. Capt. John Mawn, public information officer of Elvis's outfit, was up all night answering frantic calls from all over the world, reassuring the callers that Elvis had not been involved in the accident and was perfectly fit.

January 8, 1959, was Elvis's twenty-fourth birthday. To mark the occasion and share it with his fans, Elvis gave a telephone interview to American Bandstand host, Dick Clarke. The interview was notable mainly for its informality, with Clarke calling Elvis direct at his home in Bad Nauheim and catching him just as he came through the door at 5.30 P.M., after another day at Ray Barracks.

Elvis sounded in good form. In the course of the conversation, he confirmed that he would be discharged from the Army some time between February 20 and March 2 the following year. He would then appear in a television

special with Frank Sinatra and make another movie, appropriately entitled *GI Blues*. Asked by Clarke what he felt about appearing on TV with Sinatra, Elvis diplomatically stated that he considered it "a great honor" and that he "admired him very much."

The fans were in for another treat when pictures of Elvis giving blood appeared in newspapers around the world. This procedure was performed on Elvis and another donor, PFC George Mayers, by German Red Cross nurse Marie Everle on January 16. The whole PR exercise was overseen by Bad Nauheim's Mayor Geissler, who beamed admiringly at Elvis for the benefit of the ever-present press photographers. The other 178 GIs who also gave blood that day didn't attract quite so much attention.

When the photos were published, the German teen magazine *Bravo* reported that many of its readers had written in, enquiring if they could purchase Elvis's blood from the Red Cross in order to inject it into their own veins.

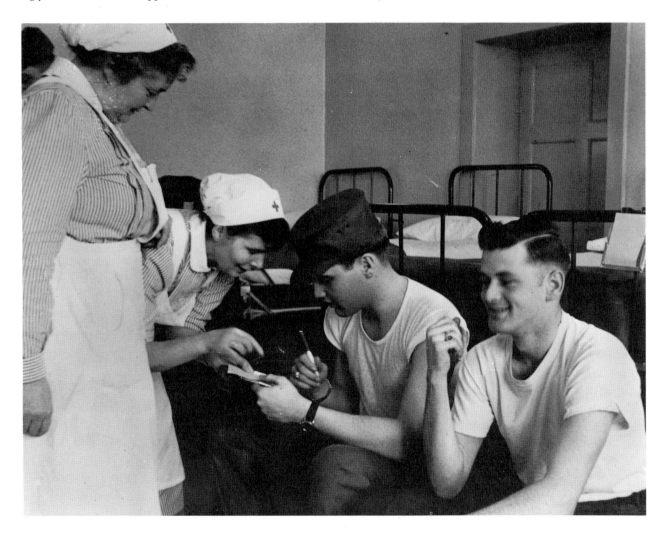

After donating blood, Elvis was deemed fit enough to sign autographs watched by Private George Mayers.

[handwritten letter]

Date February 15. 1959   Page 2 (1st after 6pm)

To whom it may concern

I was shattered to hear of the tragic accident Feb. 23 1959 in which Buddy Holly and other members of the "Star Show of Stars '59" were killed. Regarding to my ~~matter~~ ~~the~~ after third day ~~that send letters of~~ ~~folschulz of letter~~. A lot of people asked why I didn't took part at the funeral. I have to say that I'd sent a telegram of condolence to ~~the~~ Holly's in Lubback, Texas, ~~It~~ in which I'd ~~confirmed~~ stated that ~~I was not allowed to leave the post~~ there's no possibility to condolence personally as I'm not allowed to leave the post. The German press is very far behind so they didn't ~~mention the plane crash~~ took notice about what had happened. I was listening to ~~E~~ 7N station Frankfurt and ~~that~~ on the same evening they'd requested ~~after the~~ ~~gave me a call and~~ ~~requested an interview. After he talked to my~~ ~~they didn't come back to me after talking to the heads~~ of 2nd Armored Division. However, ~~because~~ I'd never met Buddy Holly personally ~~but~~ I share the grief with his family and hope that they'll find trust in God as I did after the loss of my beloved mum.

God bless

E.P.

open letter dated February 15, explaining that he had not attended the funeral because he couldn't get leave from the Army. He also complained that the German press was so "far behind", they had taken no notice of the tragedy. This handwritten letter was edited by someone unknown, possibly Vernon Presley, and the new, much shorter, ungrammatical version was typed out with the following day's date.

"I share the grief with his relatives," Elvis wrote, "and hope that they'll find trust in God as I did after the loss of my beloved Mother."

Never published, the letter only came to light three decades later.

On April 10, Ray Barracks in Friedberg was opened to the public and people flocked in just to see Elvis. Although the Army could not persuade Elvis to sing, they managed to make the most of the event by putting him in charge of the football competitions. This involved picking the teams, acting as official host, and explaining the game to the many visitors, although he did not take part in the games. Less than a week later, the Army managed to

*Above: **The letter written by Elvis on hearing of the deaths of Buddy Holly, "Big Bopper" and Ritchie Valens. The letter was badly edited, probably by Vernon.***
Right and facing page: In April 1959, Elvis was sent with a work detail to erect a war memorial in Steinfurth.

A few weeks later, on February 3, Buddy Holly, Ritchie Valens and J.P. "Big Bopper" were killed in a plane crash in Clear Lake, Iowa. Marking the beginning of the worst year in the history of rock and roll, this tragic day became known as "The Day The Music Died" and has since been immortalized in Don McLean's epic song, *American Pie*.

Elvis sent a note of condolence to Holly's parents in Lubbock, Texas, then wrote an

involve Elvis in another PR event when they sent him, as part of a work detail, to Steinfurth to help raise a memorial statue to the veterans of World War I - and, of course, to be photographed by the press while so doing.

On June 1 Elvis was promoted to Specialist Fourth Class (the equivalent of corporal), which included a raise of $22.93, taking his pay from $99.37 to $122.30 a month. His celebration consisted of a week in the Army's 97th General Hospital in Frankfurt, being treated for tonsillitis and a throat infection.

During his hospitalization, Elvis received an unexpected shock from his father: Vernon had been having an affair with Mrs. Davada "Dee" Elliot Stanley, a petite blonde, blue-eyed mother of three children and wife to Bill Stanley, a non-commissioned officer stationed at Elvis's base in Friedberg. The couple had met at the Hotel Grünewald when Dee, originally from Tennessee, called Elvis to ask him to supper: Elvis responded by inviting her to the hotel for supper instead and then he let Vernon stand in as host. Instantly attracted to the vivacious Dee, Vernon was soon visiting the Stanleys at home. He then became involved with Dee behind her husband's back and guiltily started planning to marry her.

The affair caused a scandal in Bad Nauheim. One witness, Frau Floer, then working at Foto Boelke and writing articles for the English press, guessed that something was going on when she saw Vernon more than once in the park in Bad Nauheim, walking hand-in-hand with a mysterious blonde lady.

Fans congregated persistently outside Elvis's house to photograph him and Vernon was usually willing to pose with his son or even to sign autographs. Right: Although Elvis had changed out of his uniform on the evening when this English fan visited, he went back into the house to collect his cap when she asked him to pose as a soldier.

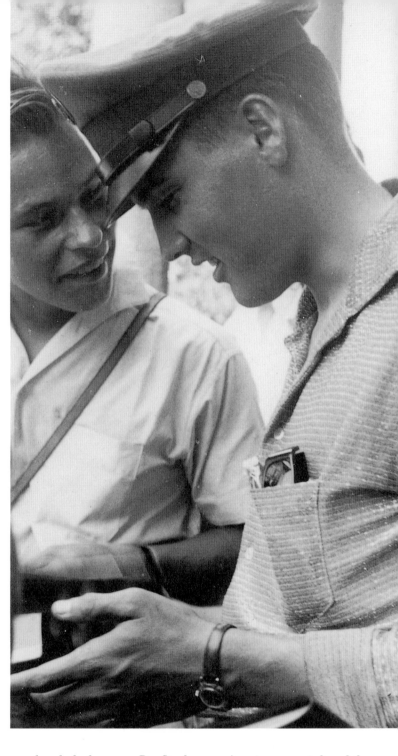

As Frau Floer knew, Vernon already had a reputation with the locals as a hard-drinking womanizer. *Bild am Sonntag* commented that "Elvis's father caused him quite a few problems" and suggested that he was quick to exploit his son's fame to his own benefit. According to their report on Vernon: "usually after a few drinks of whisky he himself signed autographs, let himself be photographed with girls. He also had a soft spot for girls." Seeing Vernon with his mysterious blonde, Frau Floer's curiosity was aroused and she looked into the matter, soon learning that the lady,

Dee Stanley, was American, married, and the mother of three healthy sons. When word of this liaison spread around the town, the elderly locals were horrified.

The situation came to a head when Elvis was visited by Vernon and Dee, who were nervously seeking his permission to marry as soon as a divorce could be arranged for Dee. Though he had often complained bitterly to friends about the affair, Elvis said, "Yes." Discharged from hospital, he learned from Elisabeth Stefaniak that Vernon had moved Dee temporarily into 14 Goethestrasse in his

absence - without telling Elvis about it. The final blow came when Vernon said he wanted to move Dee and her three sons into Graceland, the home Elvis was already viewing as a shrine to his mother.

Though Elvis generally liked Dee, he would never fully forgive his father for marrying her. Hiding his resentment, he said he was delighted and that he would add another room onto Graceland for them.

Vernon was relieved, but Elvis nurtured secret resentment, feeling exploited and shocked that his father had betrayed Gladys. This, as with so many other events in his life, caused Elvis to withdraw even more into himself, feeding his feelings of insecurity.

His charm was still there, but it was no longer natural; often it was calculated. Elvis Presley was changing.

* * *

One of those who may have suffered more than expected from Elvis's darker side was Monsieur Laurenz, a masseur who owned the prestigious De Fleur clinic in Johannesburg, South Africa. Laurenz had bombarded Elvis with literature about himself and the many famous people he had treated with his special health foods, vitamins and mud packs. Always self-conscious about his appearance, Elvis invited Laurenz to Bad Nauheim, moving him into the Rex Hotel. The plan was that he

Above left: *Elvis in his BMW. By this time he had repainted it red.*

Above and below: *A favorite place for fans to photograph Elvis was at his own front door.*

would give Elvis facial treatment and also body massage.

Laurenz arrived at Bad Nauheim on November 13 and went to work on Elvis straight away. The treatments progressed nicely for two or three weeks, with Elvis spending a couple of hours each evening alone with Monsieur Laurenz in his bedroom at Goethestrasse, his face covered in mud compound, having massages, and consuming a wide variety of Monsieur Laurenz's special vitamins and health pills.

This relationship abruptly came to an end when, one evening, in full view of Elisabeth Stefaniak, Elvis came bounding down the stairs, screaming, "That son of a bitch from South Africa is queer!" He then ordered Red and Lamar to throw Laurenz out of the house.

Lamar and the volatile Red West dragged Monsieur Laurenz, yelling and screaming, downstairs and hurled him bodily out into the street, followed by his mud packs, vitamins and other pills. The outraged Monsieur Laurenz threatened to sue Elvis. Instead of doing so, he returned the same evening, bearing a letter, several pages long, containing detailed information on all the outrageous things he claimed to have seen

going on in the house.

If Elvis paid him $15,000, he explained, the letter would not be sent to the press and he would, of course, also drop his planned lawsuit.

After deep consultation with Vernon, Red West and Lamar Fike, Elvis decided that Laurenz had no grounds to take action, legal or otherwise, and that the letter should be passed on to the Provost Marshall's Office. Shortly afterwards, Laurenz left for London where he spent some time before eventually returning to South Africa.

Exactly what happened between Elvis and Monsieur Laurenz is not known. Also not known is the nature of the supposedly incriminating evidence contained in Mr Laurenz's letter. A retrospective *Bild am Sonntag* article, dated March 27, 1960, suggests that Monsieur Laurenz was "well informed about the girls in Elvis' life." Elisabeth Stefaniak, while not passing comment on the actual allegations in the letter, states that its "contents" were true.

Either way, the press got hold of the story and had a field day. While Stefaniak has it that Red and Lamar merely threw Laurenz out of the house on the orders of Elvis, Laurenz claimed that Elvis attacked him with a knife and that Lamar and Fike, after dragging him from the house, beat him up. Certainly, shortly after the event, Laurenz turned up at the Central Bar with a bruise still on his face, and informed the owner, Elsie, that he had received it from Elvis. He then sat down and wept over his drink.

Another strange incident occurred in late December 1959 when, attempting to leave the Ray Barracks with the usual knot of autograph hunters looking on, Elvis was stopped by a guard who complained that the headlights on his car were dirty. It was part of the guard's duties to ensure that personnel leaving the base did so in vehicles safe to be driven on the public highway; he therefore refused to let Elvis go out until the lights were cleaned. Elvis was furious.

Later, when the guard was off duty, Red and Lamar paid him a visit and insisted that he accompany them to meet Elvis at 14 Geothestrasse. Intimidated, the guard went with them. After a few minutes in the house with Elvis, the guard emerged with a cloth and personally cleaned the lights. Elvis looked on, grinning.

Elvis is not likely to have threatened the guard, but probably gave him $100 or so to wipe the lamps clean, thereby restoring his dented ego and wounded public image.

Nevertheless, if he was showing signs of arrogance and a growing autocratic nature, his generosity remained unimpaired. Though many GIs begged or borrowed money from him, sometimes considerable amounts, he rarely bothered to keep track of how much

was owed, nor by whom. When warned about being exploited in this manner, he invariably replied that he "understood their needs and was glad to help them."

Also in December, he gave a cheque for $1,500 to a local orphanage, the Landesjugendenheim Steinmuehle, located near Obererlenbach/Friedberg, to enable the head to buy Christmas presents for the home's 115 children. Though Elvis had specifically requested that his name not be mentioned with regard to this, Hermann Schaub, Director of the charity group, Landswohlfahrsverbandes Hessen, proclaimed the generosity of the donation far and wide, adding that he didn't understand rock and roll, but was impressed by Elvis.

Above and left: *Elvis again caught outside his house.*

Left: *Accompanied by some young admirers, Elvis checks out the rail timetable at the station in Bad Nauheim prior to one of his out of town trips.*

Chapter 5
FOREIGN AFFAIRS

While concentrating on being a good soldier, Elvis had not been ignoring his love-life. In fact, within days of his arrival in Germany, he was dating a 17-year-old German stenographer, Margit Buergin, whom he had met in the park at Bad Homburg when out walking with Lamar Fike.

The meeting was no accident. Margit was in the company of Robert Lebeck, then well-known photographer in the German press, renowned for his superb photographs of politicians and showbusiness personalities. Thinking it would be a good idea to photograph the notorious American rock and roll star in the company of an attractive young

Above: *The pen Elvis used when signing autographs with Margit Beurgin. He can be seen holding it on the cover of* Weekend *opposite.*

woman, Lebeck asked the shapely, blonde Buergin to come with him.

Lebeck may have chosen Buergin quite deliberately, knowing that Elvis was enamored with the French actress, Brigitte Bardot, and that Buergin looked a little like her. Certainly, when the delighted Buergin was photographed with Elvis, first outside the Ritters Park Hotel, then in the nearby park where they were surrounded by a growing band of curious children and excited teenagers, the attraction between her and Elvis was instantaneous and highly visible.

Lebeck asked if he could take a photograph of Elvis with his arms around the Margit. Elvis agreed - perhaps naïvely - and the photograph was soon published worldwide, making Margit an overnight star and the subject of feverish speculation throughout the world's media.

Though Margit spoke minimal English and Elvis spoke no German at all, she and Elvis had few problems in communicating. As

was usual, Elvis initially had one of his bodyguards call her to arrange a private meeting. Thereafter, they met several times a week, sometimes in Bad Nauheim, other times at her home in Frankfurt-Eschersheim, occasionally going to the cinema, often having quiet chats in little bars around the city where they could be alone, undisturbed by fans or the press.

"She's blonde and has blue eyes," Elvis informed an Armed Forces Network reporter. "I've seen her about five times already, which is more than any other girl 'round here."

When Elvis went to Frankfurt to see Margit, which he did alone, driving his already well-known white BMW 507, he had trouble in finding somewhere to park - preferably somewhere out of sight, of the fans who would scribble, paint or scratch messages on the paintwork at every available opportunity. According to Herbert Glover of the American Forces Network, Elvis was given permission to keep his BMW in the AFN car park, with the staff ordered not to bother

him for autographs or souvenirs when he arrived or departed. Elvis would then take a taxi from the AFN building to meet Margit Buergin. He sometimes stayed overnight in Frankfurt and, according to Elisabeth Stefaniak, Margit often turned up at 14 Goethestrasse, to spend the evening.

Christened "Little Puppy" by the fans, the previously unknown Margit soon found herself in the middle of a publicity whirlwind. Practically overnight, she became the most discussed woman in Germany. Dazzled by this sudden fame, Margit soon developed ambitions to become a model or movie actress. To this end, she posed for widely syndicated pin-up pictures in which she did, indeed, look remarkably like Elvis's beloved Brigitte Bardot. She proudly displayed the wristwatch Elvis had given her, and regularly passed comments on her boyfriend to the hungry European and English-language press.

"He is shy and rarely speaks about himself," she informed reporter Mike Tomkies. "He is not at all conceited. He doesn't like to go out often. We spend evenings listening to pop records or he would play the piano and sing folk songs. I was surprised he could play the piano so well. He plays the guitar and says as little as possible about his success as a singer."

Things came to a head when a pin-up picture of Margit was published in the American soldier's magazine, *Overseas Weekly*. Elvis stopped seeing her shortly after.

Red West harbored no doubts about the situation. "She went and got herself pin-up pictures made," he told Antony Terry after the latter had interviewed Buergin, "and spread them all over the front pages as Elvis Presley's German fraulein. Elvis doesn't like that. It made him mad. He certainly liked her a lot, but after that he never saw her again."

Margit sank back into relative anonymity when Elvis, possibly feeling exploited, and certainly forced to defend his actions to Anita Wood, his girlfriend back in Memphis, informed the press that the relationship wasn't serious.

"I feel mad and humiliated," Margit complained. "All the girls who envied me so are now busy making jokes about Presley's ex-girl friend."

The relationship had lasted a few months. Years later, when living in America

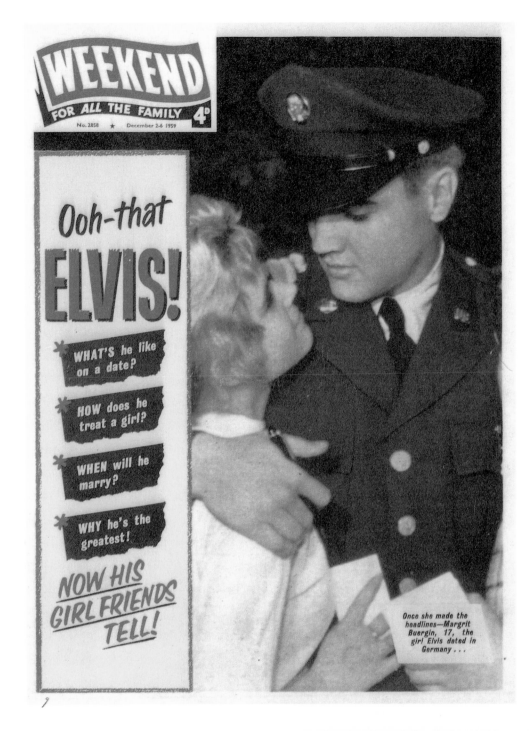

Once she made the headlines—Margrit Buergin, 17, the girl Elvis dated in Germany . . .

and still struggling to become a model and movie star, Buergin would insist that it was she who had dropped Elvis, not vice versa. He was, Margit claimed, too concerned about his image with his millions of girl fans: He took the view that he belonged to his public and could not desert them, and therefore refused to consider marriage. "I'm a corporation, not a man," Margit says Elvis told her in 1959. "Sure, I want to get married and have kids. But for me it's impossible."

* * *

Elvis was not alone for long. Shortly after dropping Margit, he was seen and photographed in the company of Vera Tschechowa, a dark-haired, delicately beautiful, 18-year-old movie starlet who claimed to be descended from the Russian playwright, Anton Chekhov. Tschechowa, already famous in her own right, having that year been voted Germany's No. 1 pin-up girl, was a lot more sophisticated than Buergin.

A romance between Germany's No. 1 starlet and America's leading rock and roll singer was something the press could not resist. Within days of the release of the first photographs of Elvis and Vera together, the reporters had worked themselves into a frenzy of speculation about the exact nature of the relationship.

Tschechowa first met Elvis when she came to Friedberg to pose with him for pub-licity shots for *Confidential* magazine. It had been arranged that Elvis would meet a child in a wheelchair and be photographed giving him presents. Having triggered a photo opportunity guaranteed to stir the emotions of their readers, the final touch, in the eyes of the media men, was to add an element of glamor. Vera Tschechowa had just completed a movie in America and, conveniently, could speak English. She was asked to pose with Elvis and the crippled child, the son of an American serviceman, in the 97th Military Hospital in Frankfurt.

"We took these horrible photographs," Vera informed close friend Toni Netzle. "Later, a journalist from Hamburg showed me the article: what terrible trash! This child bound to a wheelchair, and Elvis standing with the child. I was somewhere with the nervous parents. How awful!"

Above: *Elvis in Munich with Vera Tschechowa.* **Left and opposite:** *Elvis first met Vera at a publicity photo call with polio victim Stephen Parquett for the "March of Dimes" charity. Elvis had been involved with the charity in the US.*

On June 17, 1959, Elvis was given a ten day furlough and went on a mini-tour of Europe, accompanied by Red West and Lamar Fike. First they went by taxi from Bad Nauheim to Munich. The taxi driver was Mr Joseph Wehrheim, who had been Elvis's personal driver from the earliest days in Bad Nauheim.

When in Munich, Elvis stayed for three days with Vera Tschechowa and her mother, Ada. At the time, Vera was performing in a minor play (*The Seducer*) in the Theater unter den Arkaden, located in the Maximilianstrasse. When Elvis told Vera's mother he wanted to see the show, she reminded him that he would not understand what was being said. "That doesn't matter," Elvis replied. He then hired the whole theater and turned up for the performance in the company of two friends described by Vera as his "fat and nasty bodyguards." At first, Vera thought the theater was empty… then she saw Elvis and his bodyguards, sitting right in the front row, beaming up at her.

After the performance, Vera went with her mother, Elvis, Red and Lamar, for a meal in the exclusive Kanne restaurant in the Maximilianstrasse. They all ended up at the

Tschechowas' home in Obermenzing, with the three Americans intending to stay there for a day or two. In the event, Red and Lamar didn't last that long, being deported to the nearby Hotel Edelweiss. Ada had a very low opinion of Red and Lamar. She thought them rude and uncouth - specifically in their use of bad language, their raids on the refrigerator, and they "always had their feet on the table". She also took great exception to coming home and finding the pair lolling around drunk in her living room with everything around them in a complete mess - so she kicked them out and told them not to come back. Elvis, however, stayed on with the Tschechowas.

Above: *Elvis dining out with Vera. Lamar Fike and Red West can be seen sitting opposite them.*

Opposite: *Elvis with Vera at the Bavaria Film Studios. The original photograph had Elvis and Vera standing slightly further apart, but this print was cut and retouched to bring them together.*

Left: *In this detail from the original of the shot shown opposite, the trim on the backdrop behind ELvis can be seen. This section was cut out to bring Vera in towards Elvis. This shot was later used as a signature card by RCA.*

Opposite: *The film studio was shooting a Viking movie during Elvis and Vera's visit.*
Left and below: *Elvis with Marianne, a dancer at the Moulin Rouge club in Munich. She dedicated a special dance routine to him.*

The following evening, after Elvis and Vera had shared a pleasant day together, including a trip to the Bavaria film studios and a motor-boat ride on Lake Starnberger, Vera and some friends joined Elvis and his bodyguards on a visit to the Moulin Rouge nightclub where they were entertained by twin-dancers and strippers. Elvis clearly enjoyed being in the club, although he does look bored and listless in some of the photographs taken of him posing with a variety of dancers, nightclub staff and guests, and he visited on a number of occasions.

His behavior at the club, however, was at times dominated and dictated by his two bodyguards, according to Vera Tschechowa's friend, Toni Netzle, who was shocked by the way that Red and Lamar treated Elvis.

"That evening was a terrible experience in my memory," says Netzle, then the public relations manager for Polydor Records, "because he wasn't allowed to do anything."

According to Netzle, Elvis began to sing along with the band until one of his bodyguards told him to stop. Then he tried singing at the table, but that wasn't allowed either. Finally, he started beating out the rhythm on the table, but they stopped that as well. One of them threw a comb across the table and contemptuously told him to comb his disarrayed hair. Once, when he merely wanted to say cheers with a glass of champagne, he was told to put the glass down and drink his tomato juice instead.

This page: Elvis with twin show-girls at the Moulin Rouge and, bottom right, chatting with the band.

"He wasn't even allowed to go to the toilet by himself. I got really upset about that, because I think it's inhuman... they were really strict..."

Another witness, Elisabeth Brandin, wife of the songwriter, Walter Brandin, there to protect Vera, confirms this odd aspect of the formerly carefree, frequently aggressive Elvis: "I also remember that his guards gave him a comb and told him to comb his hair - he jumped up and did it. He had to do everything that his guards told him to do... He did it right away, without thinking, whether it would fit in that moment or not."

Looking striking in his summer uniform, Elvis poses with a guest at the Moulin Rouge.

Right: Having borrowed Elvis's jacket, Red takes advantage of his near-celebrity status.
Below: Elvis joking with Red and Lamar.
Bottom left: Lamar and Elvis with a female admirer.
Bottom right: Red with the twin show-girls.

Elvis's departure from the Tschechowa household came when, according to Herr Thomas Beyl, a close friend of the family (who claims he was told the story by Ada Tschechowa), Ada went upstairs to find Elvis and Vera together in Vera's bedroom. Elvis was then kicked out as well.

Vera, however, has consistently denied that anything occurred between her and Elvis and gives a much milder version of the story.

"After he had bothered our animals, canaries, dogs and cats long enough, my mother said to him: 'Now you better leave - there is the door. Goodbye!'"

While admitting that she was Elvis's main motivation for visiting Munich, Vera has always insisted that she was not enamored with him, had no affair with him, and,

Left and Below: *Elvis accompanied by a young woman at the Moulin Rouge.*
Bottom: *Lamar enjoying his night out at the club.*

indeed, thought little of him or his so-called bodyguards.

"They were standing around him like walls and I have to say they were belching and farting and everything that belongs to it. I believe that he never went without them, even to the toilet. I believe, also, that he was incredibly shy, a typical middle-class American boy..."

Vera also claims that Elvis had the hots for one of the girls in the Moulin Rouge and told Vera he would be spending the night in the club. She says that he turned up for breakfast the next morning, with "bits of tinsel everywhere, in his hair and his eyebrows" and that when she asked him where he had been, he only said, "I stayed there."

* * *

When Elvis finally reached Paris, arriving on June 21, he booked into the Hotel Prince de Galles, located on the Avenue George V. There, according to a room-service waiter, young ladies were seen "going in and out of Monsieur Presley's suite, in and out, like a door revolving."

When not so involved with those young ladies, Elvis found time to conduct a massive press conference in the hotel lounge where he faced the inevitable barrage of lights, cameras and microphones. Once that ordeal was over, he was free to spend his time visiting the Cafe de Paris and the Lido, a renowned, if old-fashioned, semi-nude revue theater starring the Bluebelle Girls chorus-line. There, he became friends with the black singer Nancy Holiday, who was famous in the 1950s

Right: *Elvis watching the show at the Lido club in Paris.*
Below: *Chatting with a journalist at his Paris Press conference.*

and appearing in that nightclub as her career took a downward turn. He also met the singers, George and Bert Bernard.

Looking even more handsome in his dress uniform, Elvis was photographed popping champagne. One night, according to one of the employees, when the Bernard brothers had completed their act, Elvis was dragged up on the stage, where he sang a single song, then played *Willow Weep For Me* on the piano.

"For the first time in fifteen months," Elvis told a reporter the day after, "there I was in front of an audience. Then it flew all over me, boy - sudden fear."

Red West returned to the United States shortly after visiting Munich with Elvis and Lamar Fike. He did not travel on to Paris with the group and was at the house in Bad Nauheim in June 1959 when singer Frankie Avalon dropped by to pay his respects to Elvis. Red told him that Elvis was in Paris. Another visitor to the house at this time was the British singer Cliff Richard, then widely billed as Britain's answer to Elvis Presley. Vernon was the one who broke the news on the doorstep to the disappointed Richard that Elvis was not home.

Red's abrupt departure from Germany can only really be explained by his increasingly imprudent behavior - culminating in the bullying incidents at the Moulin Rouge club in Munich. As far as Elvis was concerned, Red's presence in Germany was no longer required. Once the troublesome Red West was out of the way, Elvis was able to relax during the French leg of his trip.

This page: *Visitors to 14 Goethestrasse while Elvis was in Munich and Paris included Frankie Avalon and Cliff Richard as well as these two English journalists who were greeted on the doorstep by Vernon Presley.*

Above and opposite: *Elvis at dinner with Vera Tschechowa in Munich.*

By the time Elvis returned to Bad Nauheim on June 26 (when his latest single, *A Big Hunk O Love/My Wish Came True*, had gone to number one back home, selling over a million copies) he was at pains to emphasize that there was nothing really serious between him and Vera.

"Sure, I've got a new girlfriend," he casually explained, "But that doesn't mean marriage. We've been around together... and I've been to visit her family in Munich... but it's just good fun. All this marriage talk is nonsense."

Tschechowa all too readily agreed. Apart from the episode at her house in Munich, she may also have slighted him because of the many letters she had received from her fans, via her sixty-five watchful fan clubs, complaining that Elvis was a common, uneducated, uncouth American, not worthy of a famous starlet and descendant of Chekhov.

"I've got tired of all the fantastic stuff they write about Elvis and me," Vera complained. "It seems hard to get through with the truth." After explaining that there was no romance, that Elvis was "a pleasant boy" who had called her "Kitty Kat", and that she couldn't say more because she didn't know him well enough, she insisted that they had never been in love with each other, though: "We hope we'll be able to make films together in Hollywood." In fact, Vera's ambitions for Hollywood stardom would never be realised.

* * *

pellet from an air pistol through the centre hole of a gramophone record at five or ten yards. His favorite music right now is rock and roll by Ricky Nelson or Frankie Avalon, and he also loves cool jazz."

While expecting the fans to accept the unlikely notion of Elvis enjoying the "rock and roll" of Frankie Avalon, as well as "cool jazz" (which Elvis actually detested), the redoubtable Ingrid went on to inform the media that Elvis's favourite hide-out, when with her, was Frankfurt's smart Casino de Paris night club, where he kept a "private room."

While Vera Tschechowa may have shown some reluctance to talk about her relationship with Elvis, Ingrid Sauer, a blonde 23-year-old, displayed no such reticence. In fact, she posed for the press with only a towel wrapped around her, showing more, and talking more, than Margit Buergin ever did.

"He is so shy and he doesn't like everybody to know that he doesn't dance or drink or smoke," Ingrid said, describing Elvis to the press in November 1959. "Maybe he thinks some people would call this 'square'. But it's just that he is a quiet guy away from his guitar."

"At home," she said, "Elvis sings and plays the guitar most of the time. And his hobby is to see how many times he can get a

Ingrid insists that her first contact with Elvis was when she boldly rang and asked for a date. Though this seems as unlikely as her description of Elvis's taste in music, she also claims to have dated Elvis for nearly a year. This included frequent parties at 14 Goethestrasse, to which many of Ingrid's friends at the telephone exchange where she worked were generously invited.

"Elvis just rings up my number and asks me to bring along some girls," Ingrid explained. "He just likes company."

This page: *Elvis during his Paris press conference, joking with the press corps and showing them his rings.*

often boldly ringing the doorbell and asking to see Elvis. Perhaps because she simply wore Elvis and his bodyguards down, or because she was always there when Elvis emerged, she ended up having frequent meetings with him, often accompanying him to the local wasteground when he went there with his friends to play football.

Siegrid's first night out with Elvis came when, after being scolded by Minnie Mae and Vernon for sitting with a friend in one of Elvis's cars, Elvis emerged to reprimand her as well, but then drove her and the friend to a party at the house of another GI, Rex Harrison (not the famous stage and screen star), where drinks were served and Rex showed movies of his honeymoon. From that evening on, Siegrid met Elvis on a regular basis.

After an intoxicating three weeks, during which many photos were taken, Siegrid went back home with her mother. Whether or not she was intimately involved with Elvis, she certainly saw him again in January 1960, during a second trip to Bad Nauheim. Shortly after that brief reunion, Siegrid returned to home and school, and Elvis was shipped back to America.

Three decades later, the many photographs of Siegrid with Elvis are published here for the first time ever.

Though Ingrid Sauer insisted that she was Elvis's girlfriend, she was never photographed with him, nor mentioned by him. Siegrid Schutz, on the other hand, though seeing Elvis often and being photographed with him more than any other German girl, told few people about her relationship with him. She refused to discuss him with those who had seen them together, and therefore managed to keep her relationship with him a secret for over 30 years.

In the summer of 1959, Siegrid, then a 15-year-old, English-speaking German fan, when on a three-week holiday in Bad Nauheim with her mother, spent practically every day outside the house in Goethestrasse,

Elvis

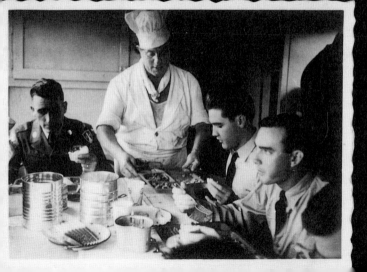

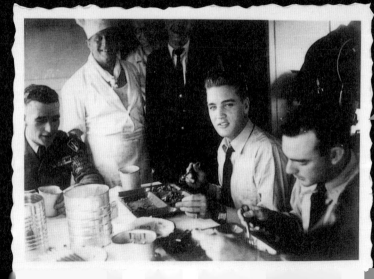

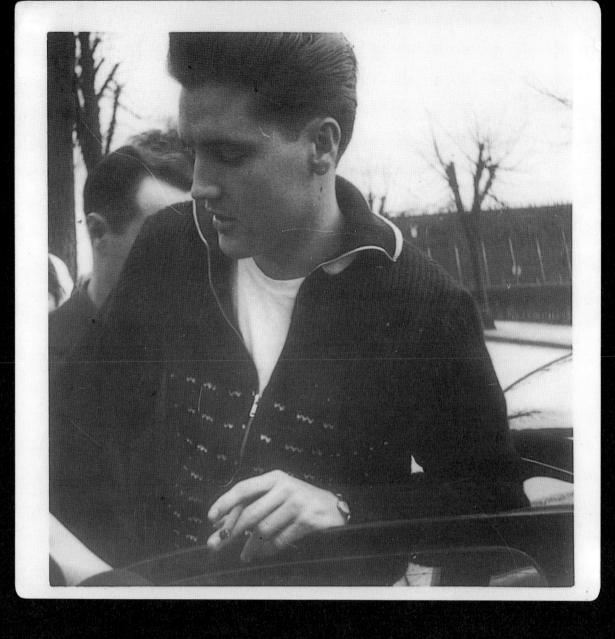

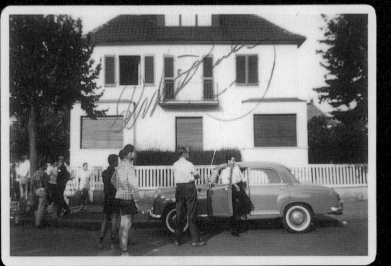

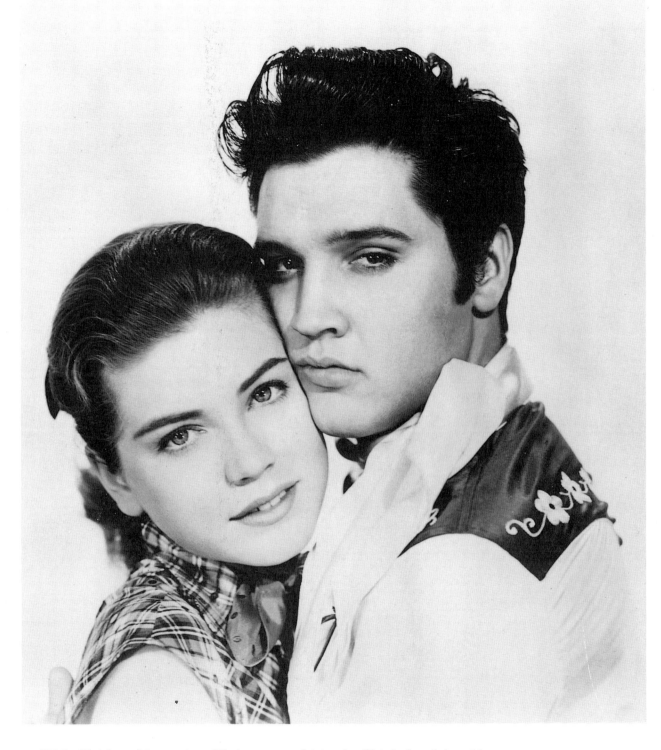

Left: *Elvis with "hot lips" Dolores Hart, his co-star in* Loving You *and* King Creole.

While Elvis's ambiguous love-life in Germany was engaging the attention of the world's press, Dolores Hart, his beautiful co-star in *Loving You* and *King Creole* - adored by many fans and thought by others to be secretly in love with Elvis - was talking to the British reporter, Mike Tomkies.

"I get postcards from Elvis in Germany, saying, 'What's doing, hot lips?'" Coming from the notably demure Dolores, this was hot stuff indeed, but she qualified it by explaining that Elvis had used that nickname ever since they had been forced to enact one of the *King Creole* kissing scenes in a temperature of 104 degrees in colorful New Orleans. As for Elvis in general, he was ". . . like a young animal. He takes care of himself like an animal does. He doesn't have much refinement, but this is part of his charm."

Not long after that interview, for reasons never explained, Dolores Hart entered a convent, where she remains to this day.

Chapter 6
PRESLEYMANIA

In June, 1959, Pim Maas, an aspiring 14-year-old rock and roll star from Holland, won an Elvis Presley contest for the best rendition of an Elvis song, thus gaining the title "The Elvis Presley of Holland". The prize was to visit Elvis in Germany.

Maas, accompanied by his parents and manager, visited Elvis two days running and sang with him in the barracks. Elvis played the guitar, Maas the piano, and together they sang *Baby I Don't Care* and *Tutti Frutti*. They reprised the latter song when the troops called for an encore.

Asked why he and Elvis had sang for the troops, Maas explained that Elvis "had promised his friends to do something for them and so he told me what to do and I did it."

Although Elvis could not be persuaded to do more than those three numbers, he did take Maas, his parents and his manager, Samuel Hemerick (incidentally the 35-year-old president of the Amsterdam Elvis Presley Fan Club, of which Pim was an ardent member)

back to 14 Goethestrasse, where he sang some gospel songs. He and Maas then sang together *That's All Right [Mama]* and *Teddy Bear*.

Maas says that Elvis was "very congenial and not the sort of person to make you feel small." Nevertheless, he became bad-tempered when a local TV station, learning about the visit, phoned to ask if they could come over to shoot the friendly gathering. After angrily refusing them, Elvis gave Maas some sound advice on how to make records and deal with the record companies, then sent him, his parents and his manager happily on their way.

The impromptu performances with Pim Maas were among the very few Elvis gave when in Germany. While he was steadfast in his refusal to join the Special Services and sing for the generals, he did perform occasionally for his fellow soldiers. On the *USS General Randall,* during the long voyage to Bremerhaven, Elvis acted as producer and director of a live revue staged for the benefit

Opposite: *Elvis meets Dutch rock and roller Pim Maas.*
Left: *Elvis with Swedish rock and roll singer, Little Gerhard. It is interesting to note that Elvis's right shoulder is missing. He was retouched out of the picture to allow it to be used as a single shot of Little Gerhard.*

of the troops. While not actually singing, he did play piano and guitar during the auditions and as backing for some of the acts. Among those Elvis auditioned, and eventually accepted for the show, was Charlie Hodge who was later to join Elvis's entourage. Elvis often sang, of course, for his guests at Goethestrasse, accompanying himself on guitar or at the piano.

Apart from such private performances, Elvis's determination not to perform officially remained resolute. By the middle of August the press was reporting that he had refused a request to perform in a NATO variety broadcast which was to be recorded in the Cologne Studios on October 7 for the British Forces Network (BFN) and which would be heard by 55,000 British troops. As the Dutch and West German forces were providing acts for the show, it was also going to be broadcast over their stations, thus doubling the number of people who would hear it. Elvis politely but firmly informed producer Alistair McDougall that he would not appear in person on any radio or TV programmes until he left the Army in March 1960.

Plans were already afoot for Elvis's return to the entertainment world once he left the Army. On August 20, 1959 Australian promoter Lee Gordon issued a press release, stating that Elvis, through Colonel Parker, had accepted £106,800 for a five or six-day concert tour of Australia, to be undertaken the following year, immediately upon his discharge from the Army. This sum, Mr Gordon announced, was the highest ever paid to any entertainer in any part of the world.

Mr Gordon's assertions were, at best, optimistic. Elvis was never to perform outside of North America and the Australian tour remained no more than a wishful promoter's dream.

Left: *Elvis at a social gathering in a neighbor's garden.*
Below: *Bemused at the sight of everyone with cameras in front of their faces, Elvis pretends to photograph the photographers.*

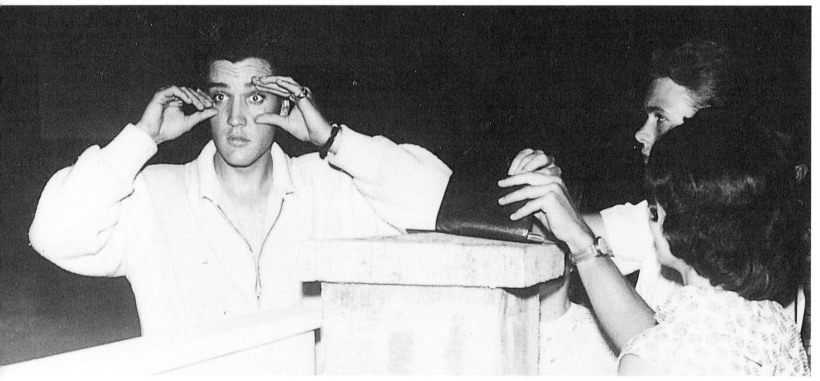

Right: Pictured with a fan near the waste ground where he played football, Elvis is wearing a scarf as he was recovering from a bout of tonsilitis.

In fact, Wallis and his enthusiastic team from Paramount Pictures had arrived in Germany on August 20, to scout locations and begin filming in Friedberg, Frankfurt, Wiesbaden, and Idstein, when Elvis was still on maneuvers.

On hearing what Wallis was up to, Elvis became depressed - more so when Wallis used tanks and troops provided by the Third Armored Division, thus arousing accusations of favoritism and exploitation. Wallis denied both charges, but that didn't soothe Elvis, who privately complained about the title and subject-matter of the movie, as well as about Wallis's blatant use of the US Army. He complained even more when Wallis contracted a 24-year old Army private, T.W. Creel, as Elvis's stand-in for the long shots, then toyed with the possibility of casting Elvis's former girlfriend, Vera Tschechowa, as one of the female leads. This did not come to pass.

Elvis's mood could not have been improved when, on October 24, he began another five-day spell in the 97th General Hospital, Frankfurt, again suffering from tonsillitis and an inflamed throat.

Visiting Elvis at home, Wallis could not fail to be surprised by the bizarre rituals Elvis had to go through on leaving and entering his own house. Eluding the crowd of fans who continued to gather outside 14 Goethestrasse was becoming increasingly problematic for Elvis. Although loathe to turn down any of his devotees who asked for autographs, he did not always have enough time to spend with them. Having discovered Elvis's ploy of leaving home via the back garden, the fans began staking out the back of the house, too. Elvis was forced to climb over the side fences and into the gardens of his neighbors, unseen by the fans - up, down, then across a garden; up, down, then across

Other plans for the rekindling of Elvis's career did have more concrete foundations, although they did not always have his permission. While Elvis was on maneuvers in Wildflecken during Operation Winter Shield in October 1959, producer Hal Wallis was in the Frankfurt area, shooting background scenes for Elvis's first post-Army movie - naturally about a GI who can sing up a storm - appropriately entitled *GI Blues*.

Elvis with film producer Hal Wallis, who started work on the first post-Army movie, GI Blues, while Elvis was still in Germany.

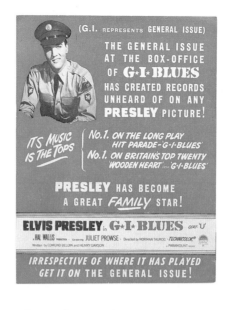

*Right: A flyer for the new Elvis movie.
Below: The film script for* Wild In The Country, *sent to Elvis for him to read through while he was still in Germany.
Bottom: A clutch of original singles from GI Blues.*

another garden - until he reached the end of the block (or, if coming home, his own house) and was again able to hop into, or out of, the car parked there by Lamar.

This worked until the neighbors realised what he was up to and either complained about the destruction of their flower beds or, more often, waylaid him, just like the fans, in order to ask for autographs or other favors. The system then became up, down, stop - up, down, stop - from one garden to the next, signing autographs *en route*, engaging in conversations and chatting to his neighbors' friends, relatives or children. Finally it became even more difficult to get in and out that way than it had been by simply going out the front. Defeated, Elvis returned to the old system of simply leaving by the front door and battling his way to his waiting car.

The car, like Frau Pieper's wooden fence and gate, was also frequently covered in messages of love, written in lipstick or ballpoint pen.

So dedicated were the fans that some became renowned locally in their own right. These included a 19-year-old blonde who phoned nightly from Cologne and made the journey every weekend to keep vigil outside. Two kids from Hanover pitched a tent a hundred yards or so from the house and stayed there until moved on by the police. A 17-year-old named Hans Jürgen Knobloch drove for six hours on his motorbike to spend one night observing the house; he then drove all the way back the next morning, getting there just in time for work. According to a columnist for

an American Army newspaper in Frankfurt, the most remarkable of the fans was a 55-year-old local spinster who dressed up in teenage clothes and twirled a hula-hoop in front of the house as a gesture of respect for her young American hero.

If anything, the British fans were even more fanatical than the German. Among the most notable was 16-year-old Jean Pearce of Priestwood Avenue, Bracknell, Berkshire, who converted her parents into Elvis fans when she persuaded them to forsake their annual holiday in Cornwall and instead make the 650-mile drive to Bad Nauheim, Germany. Arriving at night and knocking on Elvis's door, they were told that Elvis could not see them just then. However, Jean and her reluctant parents returned to 14 Goethestrasse the following morning and caught Elvis as he was leaving for another day at the army base in Friedberg. Jean was ecstatic and her parents were converted.

Even more determined was 18-year-old Melanie Burgess, of Lancing, Sussex. Melanie, a hairdresser's assistant, told her parents that she would be spending her fortnight's holiday with a penfriend. She booked into a hotel in Bad Nauheim and proceeded to spend every minute of every day of the fortnight standing outside 14 Goethestrasse, just waiting to catch a glimpse of Elvis.

"I just can't bear to be away from him," Melanie explained as she stood forlornly in the rain outside Elvis's house. "I do love him so. I feel I have known him all my life. I would do anything for him. Just to stand here and look at the window where he sleeps gives me a thrill."

Unfortunately, she was singularly unsuccessful at seeing Elvis, let alone meeting him (he must have been on maneuvers) and her vigil came to an abrupt end when the police, using a local law dealing with the welfare of young people, ordered her to leave the country within twenty-four hours.

While fans like Melanie met with mixed success in meeting their idol, their romantic hopes regarding Elvis must have been painfully shattered when he finally met his one true love and, even worse, started bringing her back to the house on a regular basis.

She was a beautiful 14-year-old named Priscilla Beaulieu.

Above right: *The GI Blues movie and album would help to re-launch Elvis's career in a totally new direction.*
Above: *Elvis is pictured here at a party in the Turnhalle in Bad Nauheim. The party was a private affair for members of his platoon.*

Chapter 7
PRISCILLA AND THE PILLS

Priscilla Ann Beaulieu is the exceptionally beautiful, dark-haired daughter of a US Navy pilot and former photographer's model. The pilot, Lieutenant James Wagner, crashed and died in 1945 when Priscilla was only five months old and living with her family in

Austin, Texas. US Air Force Major Joseph Paul Beaulieu of the Bergstrom Air Force Base, Austin, married Priscilla's mother several years after she was widowed. As Beaulieu's adopted daughter, Priscilla became the eldest child in a family of four

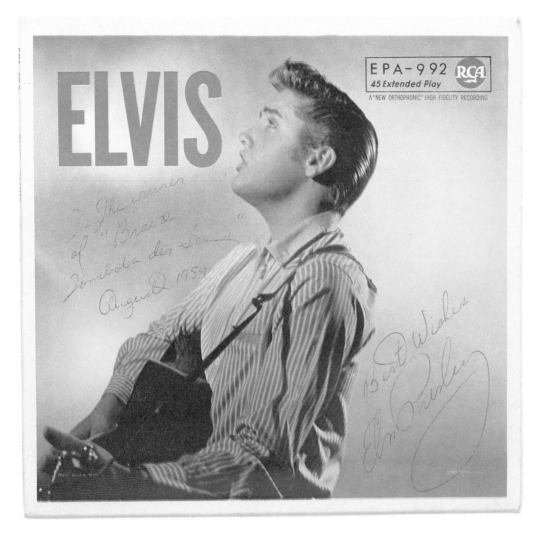

ELVIS

EPA-992 RCA
45 Extended Play
A "NEW ORTHOPHONIC" HIGH FIDELITY RECORDING

*Above: This LP was signed by Elvis
and given away to the winner of a
competition in BRAVO magazine in
August 1959.
Right: This card was a gift to
Priscilla's step-father. The
photograph seen mounted here on
the card is not the original.*

Property of US Air Force

boys and two girls.

In July 1959 Major Beaulieu was transferred from Austin, Texas to 1405 Support Squadron, stationed in Wiesbaden, about an hour's drive from Bad Nauheim. He moved his family into a house located two blocks away from the Eagle Club, an Air Force club community centre located on Paulinenstrasse 7, Wiesbaden.

Elvis was introduced to Priscilla Ann Beaulieu in the house on Goethestrasse during Priscilla's first month in Germany. The introduction came about through Currie Grant. An Airman First Class assigned to the 497th Reconnaisance Technical Squadron at Schierstein, near Wiesbaden, Grant was also a part-time manager of the Eagle Club.

By August 1959 Red West had been replaced at Goethestrasse by Cliff Gleaves, a friend who had toured the United States with Elvis during the riotous first two years of his career. Gleaves was also a struggling rockabilly singer whose real ambition was to be a stand-up comedian. As Currie Grant was in charge of the shows staged at the Eagle Club, Gleaves attached himself to him, hoping for work, and promised to introduce him to Elvis. Eventually, Currie and his wife Carol met Elvis and became regular visitors to 14 Goethestrasse. Shortly after, Cliff Gleaves moved in with the Grants at Wiesbaden and started performing in the Eagle Club.

Currie recalls that Priscilla first visited the Eagle Club with her parents towards the end of July, 1959, after which she made regular visits. Eventually learning that Currie often visited 14 Goethestrasse, he claims that she boldly asked him to introduce her to Elvis. Currie did so on a Sunday night during the second week in September, and according to him, no time was wasted.

"After Elvis met Priscilla, he took her upstairs till about 1 or 1.30 A.M. She was expected to be home by 11 or 11.30."

Priscilla's version is different, with Currie approaching her, not the other way around. She was sitting in the Eagle Club with her brother, Don, when Currie introduced himself and asked her name. When she told him, he said he was a good friend of Elvis Presley's and asked if she would like to come to his house to meet him. Rather than being thrilled by this invitation, Priscilla says she was "even more sceptical and guarded." She told Currie she would have to ask her parents. Instead of asking them, she introduced Currie to them. Eventually, the diplomatic Currie persuaded them to agree to the visit on the grounds that Priscilla was chaperoned. As Priscilla's father was also in the Air Force and knew Currie's commanding officer, Currie and his wife were designated as the chaperons. Subsequently they took Priscilla to meet Elvis.

"Well," Elvis said when he met her. "What have we here?"

Priscilla insists that she did not go upstairs with Elvis that first night, but merely into the kitchen, where Elvis introduced her to Minnie Mae, who was frying a huge pan of bacon. Over thick bacon sandwiches smothered with mustard Elvis discussed Fabian, Ricky Nelson, and the disturbing possibility that his fans might not remember who he was when he returned to the States. After a few hours, Priscilla remembers, Currie Grant pointed meaningfully to his watch and Priscilla hurried out to the waiting car, to get back home in time.

Major Beaulieu gave permission for Elvis to date his daughter, provided they be chaperoned, but no one could stop the media from speculating feverishly about Elvis and his lovely 14-year-old girlfriend.

Voted Queen of Del Valley Junior High shortly before leaving America, Priscilla was not only very beautiful (she would become a successful fashion model and actress after Elvis's death), but also unusually mature for her age. Nevertheless, the fact that she was so young may help to explain why the relationship between her and Elvis was initially romantic, and would always remain fairly unusual.

Although it was at least an hour's drive either way, often in dreadful weather, Lamar Fike drove Priscilla from her home at Wiesbaden to the house in Goethestrasse at least three or four times a week, collecting her early in the evening and not taking her back home until the early hours of the following morning. During the first few visits, Priscilla had to share Elvis with the many others gathered around the piano or record-player - including fawning young girls - but soon she and Elvis were spending most of

their evenings together in his bedroom where, instead of sex, they would indulge in pillow fights, tearful conversations about his dead mother and stillborn brother, more romantic conversations about his love and respect for Priscilla, and, eventually, heavy petting that Priscilla says failed to lead to consummation.

During this time, Priscilla learnt just how deeply Elvis had been attached to his mother and that in certain ways he blamed himself for her death. Gladys Presley had turned to drink, Elvis believed, because of her fear of losing him, either to his fans or in a war in Germany. It seemed to Priscilla that Elvis's love for, and guilt over, his mother was all-consuming, making her, even in death, the most important woman in his life. Indeed, his highest form of praise was to tell Priscilla how much his mother would have liked her. His unrelieved depression over his mother's death, Priscilla soon realized, had only been deepened by his father's involvement with Dee Stanley so soon after Gladys's death. "The thought that his father could even conceive of replacing Gladys upset Elvis terribly."

What Priscilla also sensed in Elvis was a terrible, unreachable loneliness that was given expression in his often stated concern that his period in the Army might have lost him his fans. All the fame in the world could not reassure him otherwise, but Priscilla certainly tried and often eased his mind, at least temporarily. She also supported him when he confided that he wanted to be a great actor, like his favorites, Marlon Brando and James Dean.

The relationship between Elvis and Priscilla was given a chance to breathe because most of the young girls involved with Elvis were overawed by his fame. This only made it more difficult for him to be natural with them. Priscilla, on the other hand, having lived in six different cities by the time she was eleven, was unusually sophisticated. She was able to treat him as a

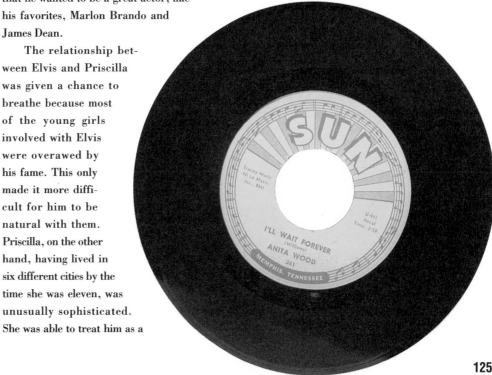

Below: *Elvis's Memphis girlfriend, Anita Wood, released this record on his original Sun record label. It was called* **I'll Wait Forever** *and she was destined to do just that.*

Right: Elvis with a fan in the driveway of his house in Bad Nauheim.
Opposite: Elvis posing in his garden in his karate suit. He was not a black belt at the time but when he later qualified to that level, he sought the permission of his instructor, Jürgen Seydel, to retouch the picture coloring the belt black.
Below: In yet another magazine competition, this time in Star-Revue, four girls won the chance to visit Elvis at home in Bad Nauheim.

Am besten gefällt ihm Conny

Die Rolläden im Erdgeschoß des Hauses Goethestraße 14 sind wegen neugieriger Passanten Tag und Nacht heruntergelassen. Daran erkennt man Elvis Presley wohnt. Als STAR-Revue-Redakteurin Eva Windmöller mit den Preisträgerinnen ihn erdunkelte, gutbürgerliche Wohnzimmer geführt wurde, ertönte vom Plattenspieler Ein Stimme: "A Fool such as I". Das Lied ist gerade seine 20. "Goldene" geworden. RCA hat von Deutschland als vor Versetzung nach einige auf Eis liegen. Sie werden sorgsam dosiert eingesetzt, bis er nächsten März, bei seiner Entlassung neue machen kann. Er kann und darf wohl auch als Soldat in Deutschland nicht produzieren. Außerdem braucht er die gewohnte Studioatmosphäre und vor allem die Band der "Jordanaires", die schon mäechen Sänger hochgespielt hat. Presleys Manager Colonel Parker tut das seine, um die Publicity drüben heiß zu halten. Er beackert die Städte mit Wiederaufführungen von Filmen, Club- und Platten-Sessions.

Den Presley-Rummel in Deutschland geben die höchsten zwei Monate. Sie haben ich aber geirrt! Tag für Tag telefonieren Reporter aus Rom, London, Paris, New York und drängen Tag für Tag kommen Waschkörbe voll Autogrammpost; Ei hat es aufgegeben, sie zu beantworten. Als er in Frankfurt den BMW kaufte — sein Vater fährt ohne Mercedes 390 —, mußte die Straße gesperrt werden.

"Ich hatte mich so auf Deutschland gefreut", seufzt er. "Aber was keine ich kennen! Den Weg von Nauheim nach Friedberg. Wenn die Boys abends tanzen gehen, kann ich aus Angst vor dem Trubel nicht mit." Von 8 bis 17 Uhr macht Presley täglich, Außendienst als Panzerschütze und Jeep-Driver. Anschließend darf er zu Nauheim, wo seine Familie dort wohnt. Mindestens zweimal die Woche geht er ins Kino, wenn er auch kaum ein Wort versteht. Am besten gefiel ihn Conny: "Sie ist eine tolle Persönlichkeit!"

Pausenlos klingelte es an der Haustür ohne Namensschild. Es kamen Autogrammjäger (die wieder weggeschickt wurden), Lieferanten, Kameraden aus der Kaserne, Freunde und die Frauen der Freunde mit ihren Babies. Außer Elvis, dem Vater und der Großmutter Minnie wohnen in der seit Februar gemieteten Villa noch die zwei "Leibwächter" Bobby West und Lamar Fike und eine deutsche Köchin. Elvis braucht Betrieb, auch im eigenen Hause. Das zwanglose Kommen und Gehen ist typisch amerikanisch. Vor März 1960 geht Presley nicht nach USA. Den Zwei-Wochen-Urlaub im Sommer will er in Paris verleben. "Nur wegen B.B.", grinste er beim Abschied.

FOTOS: STAR-REVUE / JOPPEN

Ein Tag mit ELVIS PRESLEY

Zum "Tee bei Elvis Presley" reisten die Gewinnerinnen des Preisausschreibens von STAR-Revue, Paramount und Teldec nach Bad Nauheim. "Als Soldat bekommt man Muskeln", lachte El. "Trotzdem bin ich lieber Zivilist!" Es war das erste und für lange Zeit auch letzte Mal, daß er in seinem Haus, Goethestraße 14, Teenager empfing,

VIER MÄDCHEN BEI EL

Hier wohnt El. Vorn sein weißer BMW.

Das waren die Glücklichen: Lieselotte Zeller (links neben STAR-Revue-Redakteurin Eva Windmöller), Ursula Lehmann, Rosemarie Kiel und Hannelore Bartling. Sie alle machen bei jedem Preisausschreiben mit, hatten bisher aber noch nie gewonnen.

Zum Lachen brachte El die Mädchen zu Beginn der turbulenten Cola-Party durch seine Konversation wollte, sprach er paar Brocken GI-Slang, die er lieber nicht wiedergeben wollte, spricht er ziemlich beschieden. Im gutbürgerlichen Wohnzimmer (Sofa, Ölbild mit Baumblüte, Tischrichte, zwei Sessel, Schrank und natürlich ein Klavier) hat er sich eine Art Tonstudio eingerichtet.

Wie ein Fels in der Brandung des turbulenten Haushalts wirkt Vater Vernon E. Presley (siehe Initialen auf der Krawatte). Er macht alles: Telefonate, Post, Publicity. Besucher abwimmeln, das Geschäft in USA überwachen. In seinem grimmen Mercedes verunglückte er kürzlich zwischen Nauheim und Frankfurt. Nach dem Unfall machte er sofort neue Fotos von der verbeulten Karosserie.

---

human being, an equal, even talking back when he got out of line.

"She could get away with more smart talk than the other girls," Elisabeth Stefaniak explained. "He would put them in their place real quick, but not her."

Though Priscilla seemed sure of herself and cocky with Elvis, she was actually deeply insecure about their relationship and constantly worried about his affairs with other women.

The first time he invited her up to his bedroom she was disconcerted to find several letters from his Memphis girlfriend, Anita Wood, scattered around. This was made more hurtful by the fact that Elvis and Anita were still being mentioned frequently in the press as a serious item, possibly soon to marry.

Another disturbing presence in the house was the ravishing French actress, Brigitte Bardot. At his farewell conference in Brooklyn, Elvis had told the press that he wanted-ed to visit Paris and "look up Brigitte Bardot." He never got to meet her, but he compensated for the loss by sticking a poster of her

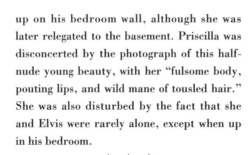

Dear Miriam –
Thanks for your lovely cards
and gifts I received during
Xmas. They are wonderful.
It takes a while to answer all
the letters.
I will answer them when I have
a few spare Moments like this.
Thanks – again for everything.
Happy Valentine's Day
Sincerely
Elvis Presley "Feb 1959"
Good luck!

Right: In February 1959 another lucky competition winner received this personal Valentine message from Elvis.
Below: The signature stamp used by Elisabeth Stefaniak, Lamar Fike and Red West when helping Elvis to answer his fan mail.

the *General Randall*.

The extrovert Esposito would gradually become Elvis's most trusted friend, book-keeper and, a decade later, foreman of his many road shows. Hodge, an accomplished country musician who had sung and played guitar with Red Foley's Smokey Mountain Boys, would go on to become Elvis's backup vocal, and on-stage valet – the one adored by the fans during the 1970s because he was responsible for handing Elvis his ice water and Gatorade, taking care of his scarves, and draping his flamboyant capes over his shoulders.

Another frequent visitor to the house was fellow GI, Rex Mansfield, inducted with Elvis at Memphis. Instead of becoming a loyal member of the Memphis Mafia, Rex was fated to earn Elvis's disapproval by marrying his secretary, Elisabeth Stefaniak, and setting up home with her in the United States.

With Elvis, Vernon, Minnie Mae, Elisabeth, Frau Pieper, Cliff Gleaves, Rex Mansfield and the three founding members of what would become known as the Memphis Mafia - Joe Esposito, Charlie Hodge and Lamar Fike - as well as a constant stream of other visitors, the house in Goethestrasse was always more than lively.

Elisabeth and Grandma Minnie Mae did the cooking between them. Elisabeth and Lamar Fike (and Red West up, until his departure) read and answered the hundreds of fan letters that arrived daily and required the expert forging of Elvis's signature on the standard replies. Eventually, a rubber signature stamp would supplement their forgery skills. Elisabeth also took care of the many, non-financial, administrative requirements while Red and Lamar performed other household duties, such as maintenance and driving, and acted as Elvis's bodyguards. Vernon was in charge of finances, keeping check of the money and doling it out, which he did with notable reluctance. Like Frau Pieper, he was sharp with his tongue, easily slighted, tight-fisted, and not very popular.

Whether alone or with friends, Elvis had a low boredom threshold that made him eat too much too often. When not eating, he would retire with his visitors to the parlor, which contained a piano, radio and record-player. An accomplished pianist, Elvis often sat at the instrument to play and sing for his

up on his bedroom wall, although she was later relegated to the basement. Priscilla was disconcerted by the photograph of this half-nude young beauty, with her "fulsome body, pouting lips, and wild mane of tousled hair." She was also disturbed by the fact that she and Elvis were rarely alone, except when up in his bedroom.

* * *

By this time the house was becoming increasingly crowded and a hectic routine had been established. Unable to remain alone for long, always craving attention, Elvis encouraged his friends to visit as often as possible, with some of them practically living in the house.

One was Joe Esposito, a second-generation Italian from Chicago, Army company clerk, and friend to Lamar Fike. Another was Charlie Hodge, an amiable GI from Decatur, Alabama, who had shipped out with Elvis on

SIDE 1: Jesus Is Mine • I'm Bound for That City
SIDE 2: I Was There When It Happened • Farther Along

THE BLACKWOOD BROTHERS QUARTET

I'M BOUND FOR THAT CITY

More than a score of years ago, the Blackwood Brothers began singing all types of gospel songs—hymns, Negro spirituals, popular religious songs and sacred holiday songs—starting on a small radio station in Mississippi. "Give the world a smile" has been their motto as they toured the country, bringing their gospel message in song to countless millions.

One of the highlights in the Blackwoods' career was the thunderous ovation extended them when they achieved the winner's spotlight on Arthur Godfrey's TV Talent Scouts show on June 14, 1954, after they sang *The Man Upstairs*. Their record of this song became one of the top selling records on the RCA Victor label. The group consisted of Bill Shaw, James

Blackwood, R. W. Blackwood and Bill Lyles, with Jack Marshall as their keyboard accompanist. A fortnight later, tragedy struck. An airplane crash killed R. W. Blackwood and Bill Lyles at Clanton, Alabama. During the dark period which followed, the survivors prayed for guidance. In order to continue the work of the Lord, baritone singer Cecil Blackwood, a younger brother, joined, along with bass singer J. D. Sumner, forming the present group. The boys are now continuing to reach troubled souls through their songs with even greater inspiration.

© by Radio Corporation of America, 1957

This Is an RCA Victor "New Orthophonic" High Fidelity Recording.

EPA 1-1488   Printed in U.S.A.

puritanical belief that fidelity was important - at least on the woman's part. Priscilla had good cause to suspect, from the way he bantered with other girls in the house, that he was being unfaithful to her.

This suspicion was only increased when, one evening, picking up his guitar, Elvis asked two visiting English girls if they had seen his guitar pick.

"It's upstairs on the table right beside your bed," one of the girls said with a smile. "I'll get it."

When the outraged Priscilla later confronted Elvis about this, he denied any relationship with the girl, giving the excuse that he'd simply mentioned how untidy his bedroom was and the girl had then offered to clean it. Naturally, Priscilla didn't believe him.

* * *

Promiscuity and over-eating were not Elvis's only outlets from boredom. He had also begun karate lessons with Jürgen Seydel, the leading instructor in Germany. Though Seydel had a large studio in nearby Bad Homburg, he started coming to 14 Goethestrasse in December 1959, to instruct Elvis personally, sometimes in the garage with a large carpet laid down, sometimes in the large living room with the furniture pushed back. Seydel later said of Elvis: "He had an incredible capacity of perception and was one of my most talented pupils."

guests - everything from *Danny Boy* to gospel and Jerry Lee Lewis. Otherwise, he would play the radio or put on some records - Gordon Stoker of Elvis's backing group, the Jordanaires, frequently sent Elvis the kind of gospel music records he found so hard to come by in Germany - while the guests talked, drank, danced, ate typical Southern food and generally fooled around playing the kind of childish games which made them so unpopular in the Hotel Grünewald.

Though Vernon and the other men often went out drinking, alcohol was rarely permitted in Elvis's presence - not even when there were guests.

The fact that the house was always filled with visitors was very frustrating for Priscilla, but the way that their mood was totally dominated by Elvis made things even worse. When he walked into the living room, everyone would stop talking. They barely dared laugh unless he did. Already his guests were like the king's courtiers, with Elvis as "King". Soon Priscilla was feeling jealous of most of the other guests, male and female.

According to Priscilla, though she and Elvis did not consummate their love in Germany, Elvis continued bedding other women. His refusal to make love to her was based not only on the fact that she was legally still a minor, but also on his old-fashioned,

Top left: *One of the many special records sent to Elvis in Germany by Gordon Stoker of the Jordanaires.*
Above: *Elvis's cap, left behind when he eventually departed from Goethestrasse.*
Below: *This silk shirt worn by Elvis was won by Karl-Heinz Schlecht in a BRAVO competition.*

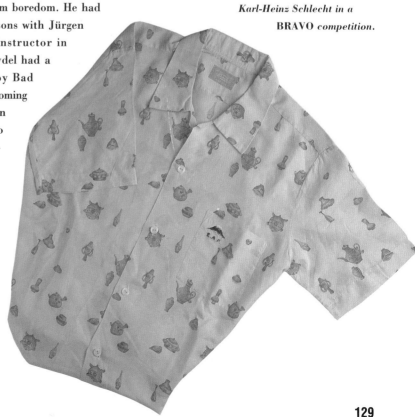

Often, when Seydel was not there, Elvis would practice with Rex Mansfield.

The karate was merely part of Elvis's growing fascination with higher states of perception and being. From the moment of his mother's death, Elvis had become obsessed with spiritual matters and often talked about them. In the Hotel Grünewald he had engaged in long discussions with the owner, Otto Schmidt, about reincarnation. Herr Schmidt had obligingly read the lifelines of Elvis's palm, and he and Elvis agreed that as the body was merely lent to one by God, one had to take care of it. Elvis took care of his body by not smoking (apart from mild cigarillos) or drinking and by the rigorous practice of Karate.

It was also during this time that Elvis started taking Dexedrine, to keep him awake during Army maneuvers, and for his forays with his growing Memphis Mafia into the nightspots of Frankfurt. For this reason, or simply because Elvis was taking them, the other guys also started taking them.

Elvis took the "Dexies" with increasing frequency and even offered them to 14-year-old Priscilla. She didn't swallow them. Instead, she kept them in a box containing her own little collection of Elvis souvenirs, including cigar-holders and personal notes he had sent her. In trying to introduce Rex Mansfield to the pills, he explained simply that they gave him energy while keeping him slim and trim. His rationalization was that they were really only appetite depressants, prescribed by doctors to millions of overweight people. Elvis believed Dexedrine to be "completely harmless", pointing out that their effects wore off quickly. In fact, Elvis's deepening depression, egomania, and paranoia, and his more frequent and increasingly violent temper tantrums, can be blamed not only on the shock of his mother's death and the intense personal pressure he was under while in Germany, but also on his increasing use of the Dexedrine pills.

The mounting stress Elvis was experiencing came not just from the Army or from his worries about his career but, ironically, also from those he gathered around him to help him shut out his problems. Elvis was constantly pestered by petty intrigues, with individuals in competition for his attention and his money. A distant aunt and uncle in East Prairie, Ohio, wanted to borrow some

Above and right: Elvis posing with fans outside his house wearing the cap featured on the previous page.

money for a house. One of his friends needed help for his parents, who were not doing well. Other soldiers in the barracks, who visited the house often, were always leaning on him … even Elisabeth Stefaniak's mother complained that he wasn't paying her daughter enough. Her salary, widely reported as being 35 Deutschmarks per week, was actually 600 Deutschmarks per month.

There were the daily conflicts between the various members of the household, with everyone fighting desperately for position in the hierarchal structure of this extended, ever changing "family" of relatives, friends, hired staff, fans, and hangers-on. This created a minefield of conflicting interests and demands through which Elvis, with little experience to guide him, had to tread carefully every day. Rarely able to relax fully in any social situation and less able to judge or trust the motives of those around him, he had become increasingly suspicious and withdrawn, isolated by his growing fame and fortune.

In the end, all Elvis wanted was a little bit of peace. The pills, therefore, may have helped him to face the more unpleasant manifestations of total, blind adulation: The jealousy, possessiveness, intrigues, and back-biting. In short, the pills became his escape route. Certainly, he was efficient at obtaining them, even running a deal with someone in the military dispensary. According to Mansfield, Elvis always had "a tremendous supply" of the drugs in his possession.

Chapter 8
ON THE LOOSE FOR THE LAST TIME

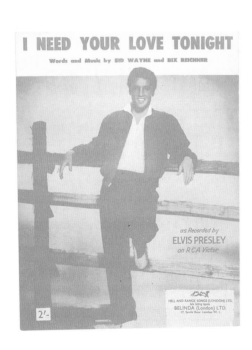

Above: *The original song sheet for* I Need Your
Love Tonight, *Elvis's nineteenth consecutive
million-selling single.*

While Elvis was on military service in Germany, his popularity throughout the rest of the world was undiminished. His single *A Fool Such As I* and its flipside, *I Need Your Love Tonight* had become his nineteenth consecutive million-selling record; his latest single, *A Big Hunk O' Love/My Wish Came True* had reached the No. 1 spot in the United States in June 1959; and two albums of mostly old tracks, *For LP Fans Only* and *A Date With Elvis*, were also very successful.

To cover the barren Christmas before Elvis's discharge, RCA repackaged the *Elvis' Christmas Album* from the previous year and released it with two more compilation sets: *50,000,000 Elvis Fans Can't Be Wrong* and *Elvis' Gold Records - Volume 2*. All were successful.

At the same time, numerous "tribute" records about him were being released; a paperback book about his Army career, *Operation Elvis*, was going into production; his first four movies were re-released; and Albert Hand produced the first editions of *Elvis Monthly*, a fan magazine that was distributed worldwide by the British Elvis Presley Fan Club.

* * *

By early January, 1960, Elvis was on holiday again, this time with Lamar Fike, Charlie Hodge and Rex Mansfield. Hardly adventurous when out of Memphis, he opted for the same mini-tour as before, again taking Josef Wehrheim's taxi from Bad Nauheim to Munich where he planned to spend a couple

of days before travelling on by train to Paris.

In Munich, Elvis either avoided, or was not invited to, the house of Vera Tschechowa and her mother but there were other familiar and more friendly haunts to revisit.

Elvis returned to his favorite Moulin Rouge club where, according to Rex Mansfield, he sat with three women in his booth while Charlie, Rex and Lamar each had a girl in separate booths.

Mansfield claims there was a fight in the club when a jealous German exchanged angry words with Mansfield's girl, then tried to drag her from his booth. Attempting to prevent this, Rex was punched in the face. This turned the normally mild Rex into "a madman" and he and the German traded more blows.

Rex maintains that Elvis stepped between him and the German, pleading with them to break it up, while secretly encouraging Rex to floor the German, whispering under his breath, "Kill him, Rex! Kill the bastard!" As this had no effect on Rex's ability to deck his opponent, Elvis grabbed the German's arms, pinned them behind his back, and held him firmly while Rex landed a good punch. Though not Queensbury rules, it worked and the German was knocked out.

This version of events is completely refuted by Charlie Hodge who remembers an incident with a German local in the nightclub but certainly never witnessed any fight. "Nothing like that ever happened in my presence," he says. "We did have one slight

Opposite and this page: Elvis posed for photographs with a variety of delighted young ladies backstage at Munich's Moulin Rouge club. Below: A Date With Elvis helped to satisfy the fans' hunger for Elvis recordings during his abscence.

Above and above left: *Elvis was more than happy to re-aquaint himself with dancer Marianne.*
Left: *Another young lady gets in on the act.*
Far left: *Having posed with almost everyone else in the club, there seemed no point in leaving out the kitchen staff!*

This page: Photographs with the Moulin Rouge's band and manager were more formal poses than those with attractive guests.

Above: *Elvis was given special tuition in Paris from Japanese karate instructor Murakami Tetsuji.*
Opposite: *Elvis with Charlie Hodge.*

had been rude to the guy and later on he went over to where the German was sitting and gave him an autograph."

They spent two whole days and nights in Munich, dividing their time solely between the Moulin Rouge or the hotel, then they took the train on to Paris, where they would stay for ten days.

Elvis and his travelling companions enjoyed complete privacy on the journey from Munich to Paris, relaxing in their own private carriage, a luxury probably achieved by Elvis having booked all the seats on that part of the train.

On arriving in Paris, the group booked into Elvis's favored Prince de Galles hotel where they were destined to spend most of their daylight hours during their stay. Although celebrities were not an uncommon sight on the streets of Paris, Elvis knew from his previous visit that it was impossible for him to wander around the city on foot without attracting an uncomfortable amount of attention. Even on an unannounced trip such as this, word would soon spread that Elvis Presley was in town. Elvis and his friends, therefore, made most of their forays out into the city at night. Fortunately, this fitted in perfectly with their leisure plans.

Elvis had just two things on his mind during this Paris trip - karate and nightclubs. Karate was to become one of his most enduring passions and in January 1960 he was fired with the enthusiasm of a gifted beginner. He was honoured that the famous Japanese karate instructor, Murakami Tetsuji, had agreed to give him special tutition in his Paris studio. This had been arranged by Jürgen Seydel, Elvis's German karate instructor who accompanied them on the Paris leg of the trip.

Elvis took karate instructions from Jürgen Seydel from December 1959 to March 1960, three or four times a week in the evening, once at Seydel's studio in Bad Homburg, thirty minutes away, but mainly in the house in Goethestrasse. Seydel, then Germany's leading karate instructor, assured Elvis that he was good enough to take more advanced lessons in the Shotokan technique with Murakami Tetsuji. This course took place at the Club Yoseikan, whose badge Elvis later wore on the sleeve of his karate suit. The day after their arrival in the French capital,

incident with a German guy in the club when he approached our table and asked us something in German. There was an embarrassing silence as none of us could really understand what he was saying. Elvis turned to us and made a joke out of it, saying something like, 'Tell him to shut up or I'll kill him.' We just laughed and the poor guy shuffled off back to his own table but Elvis was worried that we

Right: Elvis with a reporter leaving his hotel followed by Lamar.

Elvis and his friends, now accompanied by Jürgen Seydel, went to Murakami's studio, which must have come as something of a shock after the opulence of the luxurious hotel.

"We started our training (with Murakami) early in the morning," Seydel recalls. "The room was unheated and the broken glass in the windows was just covered with cardboard. We were cold in our thin karate suits and bare feet, but Elvis treated it as normal."

Murakami (now dead) was "very taken" with Elvis, admiring his seriousness and skill, and helped him to earn his 3rd Kyu, which meant he could wear the brown belt. Seydel also testifies to Elvis's increasing preoccupa-

tion with matters ethereal.

"Elvis was very willing to talk about all sorts of things," says Seydel. "When we were alone, we often talked about serious things like politics, parapsychology, character study and self-assessment. Sometimes we would sit and talk together until midnight."

The course with Murakami took place from 13-16 January, during the day. Elvis took the karate instruction extremely seriously, but once his short course with Murakami was over, he returned to his favorite Paris nightclub haunts once more.

His habit was to begin at the Lido, then move on to clubs such as the Folies Bergère,

the Moulin Rouge (not to be confused with the one in Munich), the Carousel, and the Café de Paris. Elvis particularly liked the Lido because the staff there knew him and would ensure that he wasn't bothered by the other patrons. He also loved the Bluebelle Girls, who were mainly English, and he was allowed to go backstage after the show to enjoy their company. Ever one to keep a party bubbling, he would move on with his friends and some of the girls to Le Ban Tue or to the 4 O'Clock Club, so named because it didn't open until 4. A.M.

Top: Rex Mansfield helps Elvis sew on his sergeants' stripes.
Above: Newly promoted Sergeant Presley with a fan outside 14 Goethestrasse.

Invariably, the girls remained with Elvis and the others in the Le Ban Tue or 4 O'Clock club until eight or nine in the morning, usually with a bottle or two of champagne. This was their only meal of the day.

One of the better kept secrets in Elvis's softly lit, carnation-filled suite in the hotel was a pretty, unnamed brunette. When a reporter from the British *Daily Sketch* knocked on the door for his interview: "the girl popped out, a leopard-skin hood on her head." Later, when the reporter asked Elvis who the girl was, he received a heavy-lidded gaze and the words: "Maybe I shouldn't tell you. Let's just call her Marie." Elvis then added that he had no special girl and no plans for marriage.

"I just ain't used to this high-livin' any more,' Elvis told another reporter, Rosalie Macrae, slipping out of his uniform jacket and exposing the lace frills of his white shirt. "This shirt is one thing the Army don't know about," he explained. "Officially you wear a plain white shirt with a plain starched collar. But what happens beyond the collar, well, no one knows about that." When Rosalie changed the subject by pointing out that Elvis's record sales had slipped by twenty-five percent since he left America, he replied with admirable nonchalance: "Inevitable, but we'll see what I can do about that."

The entire holiday was funded by Elvis at a cost of several thousand dollars. This included the hire of a black limousine in which they all returned to Germany: By abandoning their previous plan to travel by train, they were able to spend an extra day in Paris.

On January 20, US Army Lieutenant Colonel Thomas S. Jones, commanding officer of the Third Armed Division's 32nd Armor, announced that Private, presently Acting Sergeant, Presley had been promoted to Sergeant and placed in command of a three-man reconnaissance team (Elvis, his driver, and a machine-gunner) for the Third Armored Division's 32nd Scout Platoon. The promotion included a further raise of $22.94 per month. Elvis solemnly showed off his three stripes to the press. He subsequently performed his duties admirably, was photographed and filmed constantly while doing so, and became the darling of the conservative, middle-aged parents who had previously despised him. He also received fulsome praise from his superior officers.

"I said before that Sergeant Presley was a good soldier," Elvis's platoon leader, 1st Lieutenant Richard L. Coffman, stated with conviction, "and now I can add that he's a fine NCO." Added Elvis's company commander, Captain Hubert Childress: "Since his arrival, Presley has demonstrated leadership ability and proved himself worthy of promotion to sergeant."

As if to validate all this fulsome praise, on February 9, almost a month to the day after Elvis's twenty-fifth birthday, it was revealed in the British press that the Duchess of Windsor had become an Elvis fan. The Duke of Windsor had confided this to a fellow passenger aboard the liner *United States*, then approaching New York, adding that his wife's luggage included most of Elvis's repertoire and that one of the Duchess's favourite songs was *Hound Dog*.

A tangible manifestation of how the image of the rock and roll rebel was changing, there could be no doubt that Elvis had now acheived a status of respectablility.

Chapter 9
DEPARTURE

Elvis's eighteen-month stay in Germany was all but over. The first sign that he was due to return to the States for his discharge, came on February 12, when Minnie Mae's daughter, Delta, arrived at the house in Bad Nauheim to help her mother pack for the journey home.

Already, by mid-January, the Army brass at Friedberg were seriously concerned that getting Elvis out of Germany would be

The "Winter Shield" excercise in Wildflicken was the last Elvis would participate in before his departure from Germany.

more difficult than getting him in. Elvis had become increasingly more popular with the German teenagers and they were fearful that the crowds which gathered for his arrival at Bremerhaven would turn into a riotous mob for his departure. An official press release was issued, dated February 27, stating that contrary to earlier plans Elvis would fly back to the US instead of going by train and troop ship. On March 1, he would hold a press conference. On March 2 he would leave by plane from the military side of Frankfurt's Rhein-Main airport. To avoid any hysterical scenes at the airport, no interviews would be permitted at Rhein-Main.

Typical of the experiences of those trying to interview Elvis before his discharge was that of British journalist Harry Weaver. When he applied to interview Elvis, the US Army helpfully arranged to have him flown in one of their own planes from Heidelberg to Rose Barracks, Vilseck, where Elvis was then on maneuvers. At Rose Barracks, Weaver was given a bunk and thoughtfully issued with a pile cap, a shirt, two coats, two woolly coat linings, two pairs of trousers, suspenders, a pair of size nine overshoes, and a duffel bag. Once kitted out, he was given a pack weighing two pounds and stamped with the words PRESS KIT. It contained a map of the camp, two lists of religious services, sheets showing the whereabouts of local amenities, details of charges payable by "transient billets", a hand-out in German, a large-scale road map, an identification card, a book explaining the exercises, a concise, illustrated history of the 7th US Army, and a green flash to show he was neutral. A lieutenant was detailed to carry his duffel bag and he was taken to the supposed meeting with Sergeant Presley in a French turbo-helicopter armed with anti-tank rockets.

After all of this, the ecstatic journalist was handed a brief message from Major-General Frederic J. Brown. It said: "I'm his C.O. - and no one's interviewing Presley."

In fact, two weeks before leaving Germany Elvis gave his only official Army interview to *Stars and Stripes* writer, Wally Beene, telling him what it was like to go on maneuvers, about the fans constantly to be found outside his house in Bad Nauheim, and about how he had been treated fairly by his

Army buddies. Beene was impressed by Elvis's humility, but also noted that he bit his nails and tapped his feet a lot, displaying a great deal of nervous tension or subconscious fears.

Elvis did, indeed, have plenty to worry about. By March, when Elvis was due to be discharged, the career of Jerry Lee Lewis was in shreds, Little Richard had gone into a seminary, Buddy Holly, Ritchie Valens and the Big Bopper were dead, Gene Vincent was already on the road to ruination, and rock and roll was widely viewed as a lost cause.

His nervous condition was also due in no small way to the amount of Dexedrine he and his buddies were consuming. Rex Mansfield - always competitive with Elvis and now tormented by the fact that he was secretly planning to marry Elvis's secretary and ex-girlfriend, Elisabeth Stefaniak - admits to popping three pills per day and seeing "crawling things on the walls." Rex confesses that at one point he wanted to "start screaming and running", and Elvis must have been experiencing the same kind of torment.

A few days before he was due to leave, Elvis threw a noisy party in 14 Goethestrasse and invited lots of friends, male and female. These included his old flame Margit Buergin. When the party was over, she said goodbye to Elvis that night for the last time.

Vera Tschechowa was not seen at the party. Still living in Munich, she was resolutely pursuing her own successful career while refusing to discuss Elvis with anyone.

Elvis was due to fly home on the evening of Wednesday March 2. Two days before that event he spoiled the Army's meticulous plans for control of the press by giving an unplanned interview to journalist Peter Hopkirk in the living room of 14 Goethestrasse.

"I'll be in trouble tomorrow for talking to you," he informed Hopkirk, knowing how to win a journalist's hardened heart.

The shutters on the windows were closed, as they so often were during Elvis's time there, to prevent the fans who continued to hover outside the house from peering in.

Elvis's last press conference in Germany was a major event which the military attempted to control in a formal and precise manner.

"We're permanently besieged by teenagers," Elvis explained wearily. He was wearing his uniform with two rows of medals and swelled with pride as he held up the citation he had received from the Army earlier that day. It read: "Awarded to 53310761 Sergeant Elvis A. Presley in recognition of faithful and efficient performance of duty and for outstanding service to the US Army. A.D. 1960."

Elvis then surprised Hopkirk by blurting out that he had only one reason to be sorry about leaving Germany - and her name was Priscilla.

"Hardly anyone knows about her," he said. "She's only sixteen [sic], but she's very mature. And intelligent. I think she's the most beautiful girl I've ever seen. I've dated plenty of girls while I've been here, both German and American, but Priscilla's definitely the sharpest of them. Serious? I think I've said enough already."

Realizing that he was onto a scoop, Hopkirk quickly wired the story, thus making the name of the 14-year-old Priscilla known to the press at large. Almost immediately, more reporters headed for Wiesbaden, intent on talking to the lovely Priscilla before confronting Elvis at the press conference planned for the following day.

To make matters more intriguing, the Army then announced that Sergeant Elvis A. Presley had made a secret seventeen minute tape recording of his innermost thoughts on the Army, including those on the German girls he had met during his eighteen months in the country. The tape was being kept in a US Army safe until Elvis had made "his only public appearance since being in Germany." This was, of course, the press conference to be held the following day, Tuesday, March 1. That night, following the press conference, the secret tape recording would be relayed over the airwaves of the AFN and British Forces Network.

"He only talks - there is no singing," the Army press officer sadly revealed.

There was no singing inside the house at 14 Goethestrasse either. Elvis was packing away his collection of 2,182 gramophone recordings and the German removal men were stuffing thousands of fan letters into a dozen big sacks, for shipment back to the United States at Army expense.

The structure of the conference began to break down when the excitable press corps were allowed to move in closer and began jostling for prime position.

The press conference on March 1, took place at 9.00 A.M. in the overheated Services Club of the Third U.S. Armored Division at Friedberg. White-gloved military police with truncheons, revolvers and whistles guarded the entrance to the hall. A table with eight microphones had been set up in the hall, in front of a blue-and-red bandstand, and a troop of top brass was seated behind it. Also present was Marion Keisker, the woman rightly credited with discovering Elvis at Sun Records in Memphis, now working as assistant manager of the Armed Forces Television Network. TV and newsreel cameramen, as well as press photographers and dozens of reporters, were jammed together in front of the long table, which was bathed in the hot radiance of ten arc lights.

Capt. John J. Mawn (the Army information officer who had also handled Elvis's press relations at Fort Chaffee) opened the conference on a proper military note by reading a citation from Elvis's commanding officer, Colonel Frederic J. Brown. This made it perfectly clear that Elvis had been an "outstanding" soldier, displaying "initiative, drive, and cheerful performance of duty", thus bringing "great credit on himself, his unit, and the United States Army."

Mawn was followed by a lieutenant who explained that this was the media's last chance to photograph and talk to Sergeant Presley, since when he departed, the following day, he would do so under strict military security. "This is Sergeant Presley's firm departure time," the lieutenant announced gravely. "He will arrive at the military airport at approximately five-to-five tomorrow and will proceed directly to the aircraft."

Finally, seventeen minutes later than scheduled, Elvis appeared, wearing a sheepish grin and dressed in a hand-tailored uniform with three gold stripes. His left leg began bouncing nervously up and down the minute he took his seat behind the table. The conference began.

As expected, the questions were unspeakably banal and, as Elvis had already mastered the art of being utterly charming while saying nothing and revealing even less, there were no surprise answers either.

Asked to compare American girls with

These books were left behind when Elvis departed for America. The Belly Laughs *book was given to Lamar by Elvis. The cartoon book was a birthday present from Vernon to Elvis in 1947.*

In the back of The Office Encyclopedia, *Elvis made notes about his own records for sale in local shops and expenses issued to his entourage.*

Below: Elvis at a briefing prior to his departure.

German girls, Elvis replied, "They're both female, I guess."

Asked if he was thinking about getting married, Elvis said, "I'll have to wait till the bug bites."

Asked if the Army had "marched the wiggle" out of his system, Elvis was laconic: "I guess not. I just can't help the way I sing."

Growing back the sideburns? "A little bit, maybe, but I've got over that kick."

Was he going to write a book about his experiences? "I'm thinking about it."

Movies? "I hope they won't be rock and roll pictures. I've made four already - and you can only get away with that for so long. I'd like to do more serious roles. My ambition is to progress as an actor."

Would he find it difficult in readjusting from $200 per month to an estimated million dollars per year? "No, sir, not too difficult."

Was it true that he had been seeing a USAF Captain's daughter, named Priscilla

Left and far left: Elvis is pictured here at Goethestrasse packing for the trip home.
Below: Looking tired and drawn, Elvis attends another departure briefing.

Beaulieu? "Yes. She's about sixteen, but she's very mature for her years. I'm very fond of her, but she's just a friend. There's no big romance."

The gathered reporters were complaining loudly that some of them had press kits and others didn't. There was a slight scuffle when a German girl who had sneaked into the conference was forcibly ejected. Another girl, the 16-year-old Wilma Podesta, who lived in Gibraltar and had persuaded her mother to drive her 600 miles across Europe to see Elvis, got in by offering to carry a news photographer's camera-bag. She was rewarded with a kiss from Elvis while the TV and movie cameras whirred. The military men, having managed to maintain a disciplined atmosphere up until Elvis made his entrance, were now starting to lose control.

Finally, as the press conference ended, a proud Marion Keisker forgot military decorum and threw herself into Sergeant Presley's arms, to give him a kiss. Keisker was still being reprimanded by an irate officer even as Elvis was taking his leave of the building.

After lots of handshaking and joking with his former comrades in front of the orderly room, Elvis climbed into a car with Capt. Mawn and was driven out of the barracks. To avoid being pursued, he changed cars *en route*, transferring from the Army vehicle into a green Fleetwood, registration G7100, reportedly driven by his father but actually driven by its owner, Joseph Wehrheim. At approximately 11.40 A.M. the car arrived in Goethestrasse, where the usual knot of teenagers had swelled to a throng - all anxious for one last moment with their idol. Elvis fought his way to the door of the house, where he was met by *Film Journal* editor, Hartmut Wrede, who presented him with farewell greetings from the German fans. Elvis thanked him and disappeared inside.

Shortly after, a removal van arrived to take the rented piano back to its owner. Later, Elvis, Vernon, Minnie Mae, Lamar Fike, Cliff

Gleaves, and Elisabeth Stefaniak had their last lunch together in the house - turkey and chips. Shortly after 2.00 P.M. Elvis a car arrived to collect Elvis and he returned to the barracks. By 5.40 P.M. he was home again and signing autographs outside the house. He came to the front gate several times that evening to calm the chanting of the gathered fans by placating them with still more signatures.

That evening, reporter Donald Zec knocked on the door of the house, hoping to find out more about Elvis's mystery girlfriend, Priscilla Beaulieu. Vernon came to the door, "sleepy-eyed and yawning, wearing a tee-shirt and slacks." Asked if there was anything serious between Elvis and Priscilla, he replied: "Oh, no. He just likes being with girls. Who doesn't?" Then he closed the door in Zec's face.

In fact, Priscilla had already arrived to share her last evening in Germany with Elvis. They lay together on his bed upstairs, facing up to the fact that they were being separated, perhaps for good. Priscilla recalls that she begged Elvis for the last time to consummate their love, but again he refused, insisting that she was still too young. As usual, Priscilla was dri-

ven home to her parent's house in Wiesbaden, but this time she spent a sleepless night.

Returning to 14 Goethestrasse early the next morning, she found a large group of people milling about the living room, waiting to say goodbye to Elvis. Outside, in the drizzling rain, was "an incredible barrage of hysterical fans... in the garden, on the doorstep, on the wall." When Elvis emerged from the house for the last time, at about 11.10 A.M., those fans went wild. Protected by Vernon and Lamar Fike, Elvis forced his way through the shrieking crowd, shaking hands as he went, and was finally pushed into the car and driven off.

Elvis and his karate partner, Rex Mansfield, having come to Germany together on the *General Randall*, were due to leave together, flying from Frankfurt to Fort Dix, New Jersey via Prestwick in Scotland. From there, after their discharge, they would take the train on to Memphis.

Rex Mansfield and Elisabeth Stefaniak were secretly in love and would soon marry; but since this was unknown to Elvis, Elisabeth was in favor and scheduled to fly back to Memphis by commercial airlines in

Right and opposite:
Elvis gave an
exclusive interview
to Stars and Stripes
writer Wally Beene
two weeks before he
left Germany. Elvis
reportedly seemed
nervous and
distracted
throughout the
interview.

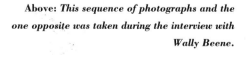

Above: This sequence of photographs and the one opposite was taken during the interview with Wally Beene.

the company of Vernon Presley, Minnie Mae, and Lamar Fike, leaving the same day as Elvis and Rex. Elisabeth helped the ailing Minnie Mae, who had had a bad case of flu, to pack for the journey. It was the first time during her stay in Germany that the hardy old lady had been taken ill. Dee Stanley had

left Germany some time before, but joined Vernon and the others during their train journey to Memphis.

Priscilla recalls that she and Elvis were driven to the airport in a chauffeured car, but given that the Army had been working since January on ways of controlling the crowds at the airport, it is not logical that they would have allowed Elvis to be driven there with his sweetheart in a private car. Also unlikely is Priscilla's recollection of the chauffeur managing to drive practically onto the runway apron, thus enabling Elvis and Priscilla to get out and kiss, before being parted by the stampeding fans.

In fact, Priscilla accompanied Elvis only as far as Ray Barracks, where Elvis's family and friends, including Elisabeth Stefaniak, were waiting to say goodbye in full view of the gathered photographers. Once the farewells had been completed, Elvis and Priscilla were separated. Elvis was taken to Frankfurt in secured military transport and Priscilla made her own way to the airport where she was obliged to join the other military families and spectators behind the guarded rope barriers.

Exactly as intimated by the lieutenant during the previous day's press conference, Elvis, with Rex Mansfield and the other homebound troops, was driven in an olive-drab Army bus from Ray Barracks, Friedberg, through the guarded gates of the Frankfurt Rhein-Main US Air Base, then direct to the waiting US Air Force Military Air Transport (MAT) airplane.

Priscilla recalls that as she and Elvis got out of the private car, parked near the plane, "cameras flashed, reporters shouted, and screaming fans pressed towards us." Elvis then held her hand and led her across the runway apron until stopped by a guard. There, Elvis gave her a hug and whispered, "Don't worry, I'll call you when I get home, Baby, promise." They were then "pulled apart as the crowd rushed in" and Priscilla was "swept away by hundreds of fans, pushing and pulling, trying to get at him."

Priscilla's account is, without doubt, a highly romanticized version recalled through the misty eyes of a teenager in love. More than one hundred German and US Air Force police had cordoned off the crowd which consisted mainly of the families of departing servicemen and US personnel stationed at the

Below: *The first post-Army LP*, Elvis Is Back, *came with a fold-out booklet of pictures of Elvis in the Army.*
Bottom: *Paradoxically, the cover of this issue of the German magazine* Film Journal *is saying goodbye. Perhaps the German LP release should have been titled* Elvis Is Gone!

air base. Various witnesses, including reporters, have confirmed that Priscilla was not only at the airport before Elvis's arrival at 4.45 P.M. but actually "staged" her farewell waves for the benefit of the photographers while Elvis was still *en route*.

After disembarking from the military bus that had brought them from Friedberg, Elvis and his Army buddies were marched straight to the plane while military police kept the crowd well back.

Priscilla, already in that crowd, broke through the security cordon and made for the plane but was escorted back behind the barrier by an MP. Elvis climbed the steps of the aircraft, but turned back just before entering the cabin, to wave either at Priscilla, the whole crowd, or both.

The crowd roared its approval.

Finally, at 5.00 P.M. on March 2, 1960, the airplane carrying Sergeant Presley rolled out onto the runway and took off. Elvis flew back to the United States and a future as extraordinary as his past. The fans waiting in America were to welcome home a man fundamentally different to the carefree young rocker they had seen proudly displaying his new uniform in Memphis.

As with so many young men whose first experience of living in unfamiliar surroundings or on foreign soil comes through military service, he had grown and matured. But the nature of Elvis's military service had led him to shoulder infinitely greater responsibilities than any of his contemporaries. His celebrity status had ensured that he could never fully relax into the comforting embrace of Army routine.

Even those he had gathered around him to help him deal with the pressures he was to face had become less of a boon than a burden. Red and Lamar had caused him more than a few headaches and Elvis felt that Vernon had betrayed his beloved mother. Gladys, he knew, would not be there to greet

him when he returned home to Gracelands.

Priscilla was also weighing heavily on his mind. As their love blossomed in Germany, he had been able to draw ever more deeply on the emotional support she had so eagerly supplied. Without her to turn to, the strain of stepping back into his superstar lifestyle would be all the more difficult to deal with. Film and recording contracts were already in place and Elvis was aware that Colonel Parker and the movie and recording industries were anxiously awaiting his return to work. While this will have gone some way to alleviate his fears about rebuilding his career, he now had to contemplate the pressure of performing again, a problem exacerbated by his own mixed emotions about the subject matter of *GI Blues*.

Although the charm and good humor for which he had become known had certainly not deserted him, the Elvis returning to America was a far more serious-minded individual than the one who had first donned his Army uniform. During his time in Germany, he had won the hearts of the older generation at home, he had been given a glimpse of how his career would develop, he had met the woman he was eventually to marry and he had taken the first steps along the road to the drug dependancy which would end his life. The first half of Elvis's life was already over, the short interval in Germany was now drawing to a close and the maelstrom that would carry him forward towards August 1977 had only just begun. ■